# FURTHER ADVENTURES OF A BLUE-EYED OJIBWAY:

## FUNNY, YOU DON'T LOOK LIKE ONE TWO

# FURTHER ADVENTURES OF A BLUE-EYED OJIBWAY:

## FUNNY, YOU DON'T LOOK LIKE ONE TWO

### By Drew Hayden Taylor

**Theytus Books Ltd.**
Penticton, BC
Canada

**Canadian Cataloguing in Publication Data**

Taylor, Drew Hayden, 1962-
  Further adventures of a blue-eyed Ojibway
  ISBN 0-919441-76-9

  1. Indians of North America--Canada--Humour. I. Title. II. Title:
Funny, you don't look like one two.
PS8589.A885F87 1999        C814'.54        C99-911087-X

ISBN 0-919441-76-9

Editor: Barb Sligl
Cover Photograph: Ken Williams
Cover and Book Design: Florene Belmore
Special Thanks: Regina (Chick) Gabriel

The publisher acknowledges the support of the Canada Council,
Department of Canadian Heritage and the British Columbia Arts
Council in the publication of this book.

# TABLE OF CONTENTS

INTRODUCTION

ADVENTURES IN INDIAN COUNTRY
(STORIES FROM THE EDGE OF TURTLE ISLAND)

LISTOMANIA
(THE BOOK OF LISTS)

A HORSE OF A DIFFERENT COLOUR
(PROS AND CONS OF BEING WHO YOU ARE)

STRANGE BEDFELLOWS
(POLITICS, SCHMOLITICS [AN ANCIENT OJIBWAY WORD])

STRAIGHT FROM THE ART
(MOVIES, PLAYS, AND BOOKS, OH MY!)

# Introduction

When I was young those many years ago, climbing trees and walkin' the roads back home on the Rez, I used to think the world was a pretty boring place. Now, as I grow older, and hopefully wiser (no letters please), I have come to realize that to any reasonably observant person, there are more interesting people, curious observations and funny incidents happening around us in a given day, to put out a hundred of these books a year. Every time I think I have nothing more to say, or that the world isn't funny anymore, the Creator proves me wrong. And I suppose if you have to be proven wrong, the Creator isn't exactly a source you can argue with. His/Her lawyers are better than mine.

Within this book are some errant thoughts and humorous dissertations on the world around us. The topics are as broad and varied as is the world, so hopefully there is a little something for everyone. And in these articles, please keep in mind that I made up very little of what you will be reading—for I am a firm believer in the simple fact that the world is a far more interesting and amusing place than I could ever create. With that in my back pocket, I will never run out of ideas. Reality is my ghost-writer.

When I put together the first collection several years ago, I was concerned that I might not be able to get the book published. More than one publisher told me the public would not be interested in the rantings of an unknown writer, let alone a Native playwright. Then Theytus, in their infinite wisdom, picked it up and, as they say, the rest is history. I was literally stunned at the response to *Funny, You Don't Look Like One*. One Native teacher at a college told me at the launch that she had been putting together a course description on Native Criticism and was worried because she didn't have a textbook. Until now. Good thing I put up with those two years of typing in high school.

That book was also responsible for me meeting my beloved, a beautiful Mohawk lady who shares my personal familiarity with the title. Though admittedly, response has not been totally positive. I received one e-mail from a Native teacher chewing me out for the "self hate of your white half and re-identify yourself in that area... get into emotional therapy or something." The first thing I always tell young people interested in writing is that people have to want other people to read your writing but to always keep in the back of your mind, you're not doing your job as a writer unless you're pissing somebody somewhere off.

Drew Hayden Taylor

# ADVENTURES IN INDIAN COUNTRY
## (STORIES FROM THE EDGE OF TURTLE ISLAND)

# Suffering from the Birthday Blues

In the space of a single month, the one leading up to my thirty-fifth birthday, my life has been turned inside out. My normal complacent existence is no more. I no longer know what's happening. Normally I like that in my life, but this time it's different. It's almost as if the world doesn't like me anymore and wants to make sure I know it. It started off like a normal enough month, with the flowering of spring and the first wearing-of-the-shorts to welcome the growing warmth and sun. Everywhere it looked like it would be a fabulous summer and I was eagerly awaiting the barbecues, bike rides, and all other assorted fun activities one expects this time of year. Especially for one's birthday.

And then the fickleness of the Creator made it known that all was going too well in the life of Drew Hayden Taylor. And evidently this had to be stopped. And stopped hard. To top it all off, he/she was very creative and enthusiastic about it and set forth with great gusto. First of all, the wonderful two-story apartment I have been living in for the last five years, located in a nice house on a beautifully treed street, is now up for sale. I may or may not be sold with the apartment. The future is uncertain, depending on who buys the house and how they feel about Native playwrights as tenants. I promise no Ojibway iambic pentameter after 10:00 P.M.

Then, to further alienate me from my home and sanctuary, my girlfriend makes the monumental decision to move out. Away. Leaving me alone. In a deserted apartment. The cruellest blow came when she even took our cat. That's cold. Now I'm catless and potentially homeless. What's this world coming to?

A year and a half ago, she convinced me to go down to the Humane Society with her and get a feline friend. She then asked me to name it, suggesting I give it some sort of Native name having to do with or referring to cats. After some thought, I named our furry friend Attawapiskat (or AttawapisCat) after a small Cree community located on James Bay. Technically the name actually has nothing to do with cats but it sounded appropriate. But that may not be what my girlfriend had in mind.

We're still good friends, getting together occasionally for dinner or brunch, and talking quite frequently on the phone. But unfortunately Attawapiskat doesn't know how to use the phone or the subway and I'm ashamed to say, I miss the little hairball-cougher. It's moments like these that make one consider the concept of "cat prostitutes." You know, cats you can hire for an hour, or however long you need them, just so you can sit there and pet them, and listen to them purr in your ear. Maybe it's an idea for which the time has come.

One would normally think that was enough in the battle against the happiness of a run-of-the-mill writer, but the trump card had yet to be played. On what I thought was an innocent Friday morning, the Board of Directors of Native Earth Performing Arts (of which I was the Artistic Director) suddenly fired, rudely and, I believe, unjustly, my general manager and asked her to pack up and get out of the office within an hour. Shocked at how this had been so horribly orchestrated, and the fact that I had not been consulted or notified in any way, shape or form (as is the usual procedure with Artistic Directors), I resigned in protest. Granted it's not as earth-shattering as the events unfolding at Eaton's, but it certainly had more of a direct impact on my life, that's for sure. I mean, I can always shop at The Bay, but there's not too many other Native theatre companies out there looking for Artistic Directors.

So, to recount: a girlfriendless and catless apartment-in-flux—one for which I may no longer be able to pay the rent, should I be allowed to stay. This is now my life. Happy thirty-fifth birthday, Drew. I may not make it to thirty-six. Youthful enthusiasm is rapidly evaporating and cynical fatalism is replacing it.

But through all this tragedy and catastrophe, I believe I have caught a glimpse of one singular truth that has been revealed in all of this chaos. I may have discovered what the Creator's personal, though ironic, gift was to me on this celebration of my birth. He/she has deemed fit to turn my life into a country-and-western song.

I would have preferred a book.

# First We Take Turtle Island,
## Then We Take Berlin

I waved good-bye to Turtle Island as my girlfriend and I left its
familiar shores and flew out over the Atlantic. We were on our way
to a country that is widely known to Aboriginal people across North
America as a land curious, intrigued, and downright infatuated with
us Injuns—a place known as Germany. It was Dawn's first trip and
my third to that fabled land where beads, fluff, feather, and leather
are always in fashion—even for those who look more German than
Native. Nobody really knows why.

Some theorize it's because of a turn-of-the-century writer
named Karl May who wrote several books romanticizing the North
American Indian. Others believe it's because Germans were once
tribal themselves, never fully conquered by even the mighty Roman
Empire. Or perhaps it's our connection to a wilderness that is practically non-existent in Europe. I promised one Teutonic woman I
would kiss a squirrel for her.

We were attending a Canadian Literary Festival in Berlin,
with a lecture/reading tour to follow, to support the recent publication of my seventh book, a collection of short stories called *Fearless
Warriors*. The tour consisted of stops at six universities, spread
across much of the Northern part of the country, all with significant
Canadian/Native Studies programs.

During much of the trip, we had the opportunity to play
tourist. One of the things we noticed was how much people over
there smoked. In Canada, we've all gotten used to (except for the
smokers of course) to not being able to smoke in any government
building, restaurant, university, airport, train station, elevator, bathroom, closet, refrigerator, etc. (bingo halls notwithstanding). In
Germany, smoking is still socially acceptable. Boy, is it acceptable!

Let's see... as tourists we had a hamburger in Hamburg, but,

5

unfortunately, didn't have the time for a frankfurter in Frankfurt or a berliner in Berlin (which is actually a type of glazed donut, minus the hole—I stored these in my wallet).

More interestingly, since the reunification of the country in 1989, massive building construction and renovations have taken over the skyline of the country. In Berlin alone, I counted at least twenty-three huge construction cranes hovering over an eight-block radius. The running joke in the country is that the crane is now the National Bird of Germany. And if I'm not mistaken, isn't the crane or heron one of the clans of the Iroquois Confederacy—famous for its Mohawk ironworkers? A conspiracy... I wonder?

In Rostock, located along the Baltic Sea in the north part of what was once East Berlin, we were taken out by a teacher and her boyfriend to sample some of the local establishments the town had to offer. It was a cute little town, with an adorable traditional (by European standards) town square decorated for its yearly Christmas market. Everything with a yule-tide nature could be found and bought. It was very Heidi-esque.

Except when we found ourselves in an ancient basement dancing club, crawling with students from the nearby university, all smoking heavily. Evidently this was a student hang-out/pub, and we had to pretend to be part of their ensemble as they (and we) danced to 80s music, like I remember dancing to 50s music. I felt old.

And crouching in that low basement, I couldn't help thinking how strange life is. Here I was, in the labyrinth-like basement of some building older than most of Canada (politically and architec-turally), on a book tour of Germany (East Germany, to make it weirder), surrounded by students who were studying Canadian Studies... And to think I always thought I'd end up working at the Band Office embezzling money from the Department of Indian Affairs. Who'd a thunk it?

In many of the stores lining the sidewalks of Berlin, Osnabruck, Kiel, Dusseldorf, etc., it wasn't hard to find such things as the omnipresent dreamcatchers (I guess it doesn't matter if you dream in German) and day-timers with pictures of some Native guy with "Indianer 1999" written under his chin. Maybe that was his sta-tus card number?

In Greifswald, Dawn was presented with a beautiful, beaded

deerskin purse by a German teacher. The professor had beaded it herself and it looked as authentic as any I had seen in my more domestic travels. I just hope the Germans don't end up doing with beading what the Japanese did with cars and cameras.

In our travels we also discovered several plaster busts of Indians, never donning less than three large feathers. I knew we forgot to pack something. Practically everywhere we went there were posters saying "Kanada" in large letters, showing a picturesque shot of the Rockies with a Native Elder in full regalia, standing in the foreground and looking off into the distance. We saw these posters on posts, walls, and fences, but we never did figure out what they were advertising. That you can get a Native Elder cheap in "Kanada?"

In one restaurant, we saw a tall blonde man sporting a "Mohawk haircut," wearing a grey-and-white camouflage bomber jacket. Then I remembered hearing something about an autobahn (a German highway) being blockaded or something.

Another fascinating aspect of Germany was the amount of good quality beer and wine. After all, this is a country famous for both.

Hey... wait a minute... beer and wine, vast amounts of smoking, dreamcatchers, Mohawk haircuts and camouflage outfits, beaded pouches, pictures of Indians everywhere... maybe we didn't go to Germany. Maybe we just went home for the weekend instead.

Nah, I don't think so. At home we don't talk about Native literature nearly as much as they do in Germany. Actually, upon reflection, I think that says something quite sad.

# Wherefore Art Thou Passamaquoddy?

On the east coast of Canada exists a little-known enigmatic phenomenon, quite similar to the famous Bermuda Triangle. Except, in this case, no ships and planes disappear, just people. Multitudes of innocent people, lost somewhere, often caused by really stupid planning. This phenomenon is called... the Maritime Triangle.

First, Newfoundland's Beothuk Indians were hunted to extinction in the mid-1800s. Gone, but not forgotten. Then, more recently, entire generations of fishermen, both Native and non-Native—once thriving up and down the coast—have become a memory. And now, an Aboriginal nation is fighting furiously to maintain and prove their very existence. To paraphrase the poet Dylan Thomas's words, do not expect these people to go quietly into the night.

The place: New Brunswick. The People: an Aboriginal nation that once had land that included a sizable chunk of the eastern Canadian and American seaboards. They were called the Passamaquoddy. The name has a nice ring to it. The issue: according to various municipal and federal governments in Canada, the Passamaquoddy don't exist. The irony: they do—there are approximately two hundred Passamaquoddy, at the very least—and our governments are bending over backward to ignore them, or pretend they aren't really there, because of the eight-billion-dollar tab that's owed to the Passamaquoddy.

So, with all this talk on the airwaves about Native people being accountable for debts the Reserve Chief and Councils run up, let's put the moccasin on the other foot and see how badly that stinks.

First, a little background: the Passamaquoddy have lived in that area for a very, very long time, according to substantial archeological evidence that includes a rubbish pile of seashells and the remnants of a Native dwelling pit that are at least two thousand years old.

But according to officials in St. Andrews, New Brunswick, this doesn't prove anything. Okay, how about the fact that St. Andrews sits on Passamaquoddy Bay? You would think that might tell the townspeople something. But that's probably just a little too logical.

How much more silly could this get, you may ask? I have it on good authority—an American Passamaquoddy, in fact—that when any Passamaquoddy goes fishing in the bay named after the Passamaquoddy nation, he or she will occasionally end up in Canadian waters. But the Canadian Coast Guard seems to "close its eyes" and tell its American counterpart that "they didn't see a boat," because these people "don't exist," and therefore they could not possibly be out there in a boat. It also sounds much like the same policy the Liberals have with the separatists in Quebec.

So, as a result of all these head-in-the-sand policies, the Passamaquoddy in St. Andrews don't have a Reserve on their ancestral land, let alone simple recognition. What they do have is an I.O.U. amounting to several billion dollars in rent owed them on the land that "they never existed on."

In the 1780s, American Loyalists fleeing the Revolution in the States showed up on the Passamaquoddy's doorstep looking for refuge, offering to pay twenty-five pounds a year for the privilege of hanging around. The Passamaquoddy, being the wonderful and kind people they are, agreed and St. Andrews was born. No sooner had the first log cabin gone up, then the American Loyalists decided not to pay for the privilege. Sound familiar? "Screw them," I believe, would be the modern translation. So two-hundred-odd years later, that twenty-five pounds a year, with a conservative interest rate of seven percent, would be worth approximately eight billion Canadian dollars. If I owed that much money, I would be pretty tempted to pretend the Passamaquoddy don't exist. The Passamawho?

The true irony of the situation, in all fairness to St. Andrews, is that the town has, I will admit, recognized one, lone, Passamaquoddy. Of course, it took a court battle to do it. His name is Hugh Akagi. A 1993 court settlement guaranteed him 4.9 acres of the property where his family has lived for many years. There he sits in his two-story house, overlooking Passamaquoddy Bay towards Maine, where his people are recognized. It almost sounds like displaced Cubans living in Miami.

9

The bottom line: the Passamaquoddy want sixty acres of undeveloped land to re-establish their nation in a context that both the Canadian and New Brunswick governments will recognize and honour. So, I guess the basic decision is whether to hand over eight billion dollars or sixty acres of land the town of St. Andrews isn't doing anything with.

Come on. This is the Maritimes. They eat a lot of fish there. Fish is supposed to be brain food. This shouldn't be a hard decision.

# Recess is Over

When I was a teenager, there was one thing, above all others, that always annoyed the hell out of me about high school. It's a rather innocuous little thing, but then again, so is a thistle. Year after year, semester after semester, teacher after teacher would always scribble down on report card after report card, "Drew could try harder." To this day I still find that term a tad presumptuous.

Maybe I could have tried harder, and maybe I couldn't. I didn't care. But there is one thing I have gradually become sure of over the years, and it has nothing to do with school: God has a sense of humour.

On November 1, 1996, I received an honour that was tinged with both irony and unexpected graciousness. My old high school— the doorstep of which I have not darkened for sixteen years—invited me back to participate in the dedication of a "Wall of Fame" within its hallowed halls. It seems that me and seven other former alumni from Lakefield District Secondary School (not the private school where Prince Andrew went, but the public school where Drew Hayden Taylor went, and where it was rumoured he didn't try hard enough) were the first to be inducted into this new and distinguished club.

I am included in this select group for my work in the arts. I am a playwright (though some might argue that) and run a Native theatre company. And it was the General Manager of that same theatre company, Eva Nell, who posed the interesting, yet philosophically disturbing, question that brought about these ruminations.

Over tea one afternoon (we are a civilized Native theatre company), Eva asked me if I enjoyed my years at Lakefield high school. I thought about it seriously for a moment before answering.

"Not really." I am nothing if not honest.

I mean, I'm not phobic or neurotic about it. I don't break out

11

into a cold sweat when I smell chalk dust or feel my bowels clench at the sight of row after row of lockers. Like most people, it merely brings back memories of that time period when most adolescents are trying to figure out who they are. And high school has got to be the worst place to do that in, what with all the peer pressure, academic pressure, cafeteria food, teachers who think they're doing you a favour by making you look up a word instead of just helping you spell the damn thing.

In my life I've met six or eight people who admit they were actually born in the city of Toronto, instead of having moved there. I think I have met about the same number of people who say they actually enjoyed their years of secondary school education. Maybe they're the same people. I don't know.

All I know is that I now went back to the school where I had faced so much trauma to be honoured. I saw the teacher who failed me in grade eleven French. My revenge? My grade-seven level "Où est la salle de bains" got me through six hours in the Charles De Gaulle Airport in Paris, France. Who needs a grade-11 French credit with that under your belt?

I once asked my grade-10 English teacher if a person could make a living as a creative writer in Canada. At that particular moment, he was digging through a filing cabinet looking for something. Without looking up, he muttered "Not really." It wasn't until almost ten years later that I started writing again.

Since I am telling the truth here, I will fully admit, without hesitation or embarrassment, that... in high school... I was somewhat of... a geek. Picture this: the library club, the yearbook committee, no sports, and being able to name all the classic *Star Trek* episodes by year, guest star, and writer. I was seen and acknowledged as a geek. Teased and ignored—if it's possible to be both teased and ignored?

There was one problem with the "Wall of Fame" though, and it was a serious one. Up until the last minute, there was a good chance that I might not be able to attend the dedication ceremony on that auspicious Friday night. My fifth book, *Funny, You Don't Look Like One*, had just been released and my publisher wanted me to go on a book tour across western Canada. And at the same time, I was organizing a playwrights' festival, "Weesageechak Begins to Dance," for my theatre company, Native Earth Performing Arts. Also, a play of mine, *Toronto at Dreamer's Rock*, was scheduled to start rehearsal in Edmonton the week before my induction ceremony, and I was afraid I might be needed for that.

But as luck would have it, everything came together and I found myself treading the halls of my alma mater. I couldn't help thinking that Lakefield District Secondary School came pretty close to partying without me. But maybe Drew did try a little harder.

# Rendez-vous with Rama

The last time I was in the Ojibway community of Rama, I was on tour with the Native Theatre School, officially listed as their "photographer." It was back in the days of practically unlimited funding, and the school had more money to spend than they had expenses, so I was invited along for the ride.

One of the performance stops for the theatre school was the small, quiet community of Rama, beautifully nestled on the shores of Lake Couchiching. While there, the troupe was offered the opportunity of staying at the brand new theme park that the village was experimenting with. It was called, and I kid you not, Ojibway World. Picture it in your mind. This representation of an authentic Ojibway community from centuries ago contained real authentic Plains Cree teepees, Iroquois corn crushers, and all sorts of wildly interpretive buckskin outfits of no definable culture. I spent three nights sleeping in a teepee by the lake. If not accurate, it was at least fun. That was back in the mid-80s.

A decade later, after a long absence, I paid another visit to the community of Rama. Ojibway World was long gone. In its place was a new theme park of sorts. It is called, in case you've been living in a cave for the last while, Casino Rama. Purely on a whim, I decided to pay a visit to this new establishment to see what all the excitement was about. This is a journal of my visit.

*9:05 P.M.* Arrive at the casino. It looks amazing, like an Aztec temple rising out of the darkness. I am amazed. So are the other people in the shuttlebus. One white woman to my right marvels aloud at the aboriginal paintings decoratively placed on the side of the building, "Pretty native, eh?" How quintessentially Canadian.

*9:07 P.M.* Enter the casino. A highly decorative, big square building. I am immediately overwhelmed with noise from every direction, multitudes of people milling about, and flashing lights

14

everywhere. A Native Honest Ed's. An expensive Native Honest Ed's.

*9:12 P.M.* I realize I am in contradiction of normal casino rules: I have an empty wallet going into the casino instead of coming out. I search for a money machine. Grab something to read from the top of the machine while I wait. It is a credit application. Beside the Instabank machine is a poster with an ad and phone number for a local version of Gambler's Anonymous. Evidently all the bases were covered.

*9:15 P.M.* Already getting the gambling fever. Cash-in my first twenty-dollar bill and receive ten dollars' worth of twenty-five-cent tokens and ten dollars' worth of one-dollar tokens for the slot machines. Pyschology lesson #1: casinos do not have clocks or windows so that patrons are not aware of the time of day and thus lose track of time while consumed with gambling. Psychology lesson #2: there's a reason for the tokens instead of real money. Subconsciously, the player thinks he/she's not playing with real money, only pretend money, and therefore does not realize how much he/she is losing. I realize this but choose to ignore it. Psychology lesson #3: psychology lessons #1 and #2 have worked. I survey the killing fields. I am armed and ready.

*9:20 P.M.* Looking for the slot machine with the proper karma, I wander through aisle after aisle of the one-armed bandits. I notice there is not one straight aisle leading from one side of the building to the other. Every aisle, after twenty feet or more, has another strategically placed machine baring your way, so that, as you go around it, you might feel the urge to stop, put a token in, and pull the handle. Make a mental note to myself: less analyzing, more playing.

*9:25 P.M.* Still scouting the terrain, I notice all the brown faces working the tables as dealers, roaming around as security personnel, and preparing food as the kitchen staff. There are familiar faces amongst these uniformed Aboriginals. I even meet one security guard from my Reserve. He's better dressed than I've ever seen him. I wonder how much further up the corporate ladder these brown faces extend.

*9:27 P.M.* I pass the all-you-can-eat buffet. Not being one to turn down a challenge, I decide to take up the thrown gauntlet. I enter this restaurant, located on an Indian Reserve, in a supposedly Indian casino, staffed by Indian cooks and food-service people, expecting some good old-fashioned Indian food. I settle for bow-tie pasta in a pepper-corn cream sauce, veal in a red-wine sauce, little red potatoes, grilled vegetables, cream-of-mushroom soup, and a bagel. All the stuff my Reserve Mom used to make for me. About the only thing vaguely Native is corn. Well it's better than nothing. To salute my Aboriginal heritage, I have two helping of the corn (although, according to a commercial I saw as a kid, we used to call it maize).

*9:52 P.M.* Bloated but content, I leave the restaurant with a healthy food-filled glow, thankful for our Aboriginal forefathers' creation of merlot. As I bask in the glow, I get my first chance to take a good, long look at the clientele of this new casino. I see a young white guy with long dirty blond hair, dressed in a Metallica T-shirt, playing a slot machine. Near him, playing another slot machine, is a woman exquisitely dressed in a pseudo-velvet, aqua-green, tight-fitting dress, complete with a feathered hat and plunging cleavage (not that I noticed). Milling about in the crowds is a vast number of people of Asian decent, particularly around the baccarat table. It takes all kinds to gamble I guess. If anything, Native gamblers seem to be the definite minority. It was my turn to upset the ratio.

*9:55 P.M.* Concoct a new gambling game for the Casino. It's called the Treaty Table. Just step up, sign a treaty, and see what happens. The biggest crap shoot on the continent.

*9:57 P.M.* Realize that I've been here almost fifty minutes, mostly sightseeing and eating. Time to get serious. I put my first token in a slot machine. Pull the handle and feel the electricity from the machine flow through my arm and into my soul. I get two bars and a seven. In other words: nothing. Much like losing your virginity; the anticipation is not worth the disappointment. But rallying myself, I feel that the next token will pay my phone bill. Or maybe the token after that. Definitely the next one. After the fifth token I understand the addictive feel these machines can generate. I take my rent money and hide it far down in my underwear where I cannot get at it. I spend the rest of the evening worrying about paper-cuts.

*10:15 P.M.* Lost my first twenty dollars. Not lost exactly. I know where the money is. "Finished" would be the more correct term; I finished my first twenty dollars. Like everybody else who has been to a casino with dreams of winning, I have a system. I carry two buckets with me—one for the money I play, the other for the win-

16

nings I plan to take home. And I never mix the two up. It's been my experience that most people loose everything when they play everything. Also, once I win at one machine, I move on to another. I run out of tokens from my original twenty dollars and resist the temptation to play with my winnings. Instead, I press the service button conveniently placed on the front of the slot machine. Amazingly soon, a man appears, ready to transform my next twenty into usable tokens. If only I could get this service in a restaurant.

*10:21 P.M.* Stretching after having sat in a chair for twenty minutes, I find myself looking upwards and discover, much to my surprise, the largest dreamcatcher I have ever seen. It must measure a good thirty feet across. And it has a myriad of colourful laser beams radiating out of the feathered centre, splashing the walls of the casino with fantastic designs. It is both the tackiest and, strangely enough, the most beautiful thing I have seen in a while. Obviously I need to get out more.

*10:31 P.M.* Decide to investigate the blackjack table—the one form of poker I consider myself to be quite good at. I find a seat, pull out some money, and ask for twenty dollars' worth of chips. I am quickly told there is a twenty-five-dollar minimum at the table. I leave with my tail between my legs. I suffer the same rejection at the roulette table, though there is supposedly one table with a fifteen-dollar minimum, referred to as the "poverty table." High-roller Drew goes back to the slot machines where it will hopefully take him a bit longer than thirty seconds to lose twenty-five dollars.

*10:44 P.M.* Can hear music playing off in the distance. Live music. Exploring, I find a small bar with a band on stage. I rub my eyes in disbelief. It is the Blues Brothers, or reasonable facsimiles thereof—nearly identical look-a-likes of Dan Ackroyd and John Belushi. They're dancing and singing up a storm. I spot two cousins audience whom I haven't seen in at least a year. They're drinking beer; I have a glass of merlot in my hand. Feeling out of place, I revert back to my younger days on the Reserve and order a rye-and-Coke, the drink I was weaned on, for old times' sake. Forgot how sweet it can be. We listen to the band for a while and learn that they have been performing here for forty-seven days straight, doing at least five shows a day. That comes out to about two hundred thirty-five shows in total. They are still remarkably fresh and invigorating

17

for such a heavy schedule.

*11:20 P.M.* The show is over and I decide to hit the tables one last time. I get my remaining bucket of tokens and decide to take no prisoners. I want to be the first to break the bank at Rama. However, doing that on twenty-five-cent slot machines is proving to be somewhat difficult. But I am an optimist. I run a theatre company, I have to be.

*11:55 P.M.* The night is drawing to a close. It is time to survey the damage I have done, and see if my system works. All in all, I invested seventy dollars into Casino Rama. In my winnings' bucket, I count eighty-four dollars. I have made a fourteen-dollar profit. I am smug. Of course, that's not including all the wine, the dinner, the tips, and the hotel room I rented for the night. I came to the former home of Ojibway World with hopes of funding my theatre company's next great award-winning production. Instead, fourteen dollars will just about pay for a one-way bus ticket to Toronto from Orillia. Maybe next time. I will just have to refine my system.

# Keynote Address for The Fourth Provincial Aboriginal Education Conference

First of all, let me begin by offering my greetings and a hearty Ojibway *ahneen* to the Nation whose territory I am standing on for allowing me to be a part of this important event. And secondly, I'd like to thank the planning committee of The Fourth Provincial Aboriginal Education Conference for inviting me to be here with you tonight. It's not often a blue-eyed Ojibway from the East gets invited to address such a distinguished group of educators. Yes, I mean you. It's almost enough to make me regret not having gone to university. See, you've already made my mother very happy.

When I received the invitation to speak here tonight, at first I was mystified. I will admit I thought I was the wrong choice for such an event because, as I have already stated, I made the decision not to go to university. I believed, at that time, that as a writer, you should not have to spend three or four years in a university to learn how to tell a good story. I thought this because all of the good storytellers I knew as a youth had never gone to university, and yet could weave wonderful tales of magic and humour.

Ah, the foolishness of youth. If I knew way back then what I know now, I would have done two things differently. First of all, I would have told myself not to invest so much money in disco records. They make great shingles, by the way. And secondly, and most importantly, I would have definitely furthered my pursuit of education, for unless one knows as much as they can about the world around them, they cannot fully appreciate the world in them.

In one of my "Theatre for Young Audiences" plays, called *Toronto at Dreamer's Rock*, I illustrate this point. The play is about three sixteen-year-old Native boys: one from four hundred years in the past, one from our time, and one from one hundred years in the future. The present-day boy complains about what he is learning

19

at school.

Michael, the boy from the future, says: "Obviously you don't like school."

Rusty, the boy from our time, responds: "Nothing gets past you Sherlock. It's just that I have a problem trying to figure out why I should care when Napoleon became the Emperor of France."

Michael, a futuristic bookworm, replies: "1799, I believe."

Keesic, who has arrived from four centuries ago, before there were any white people around Lake Huron, asks: "Who is this Napoleon?"

Rusty says: "Some French guy."

The curious Keesic responds: "What's a French guy?"

Michael interjects wisely with: "All knowledge matters. In order for the mind to grow, it must consume a variety of subjects. Your mind is just like your body, if you only eat one type of food, you die."

Unaffected, Rusty says "My mother's been living on Kraft Dinner for the past ten years and she's still kicking."

Ignoring him, Keesic asks: "Will Rusty ever need this knowledge of Napoleon?"

And finally Michael ends the discussion by saying: "Granted, he may never find a practical use for such knowledge, but it could influence other thoughts he may have."

Now the reason I am quoting myself tonight is, first off, I can be reasonably sure I have the source material correct. And secondly, almost ten years after I wrote that little exchange, I believe in it more and more. Education is more than a solitary collection of information islands in some fathomless sea of knowledge. One of the truest journeys in life is to continuously add to those islands, because those islands will hopefully grow to become a solid landmass, and even a continent. With every book I read, or journey I take, I am working towards building up that very Earth. It has been said that an individual must have firm ground to stand on before they can reach for the sky. And unfortunately, I know so many people who still live on just islands. But leave it to a playwright to throw a metaphor about indiscriminately.

Had I paid more attention in school, I would have known that Napoleon wasn't crowned Emperor of France till 1804. He merely orchestrated a *coup d'etat* in 1799. Oh well, we all live and learn. Add one more island to the archipelago.

We as First Nations people, are pursuing an admirable and exciting, though difficult, road. The journey has come full circle. Where once we, as individual Nations, were responsible for the education of our young, we now remember that one day that responsibility was taken away from us. As the Creator would have it, we are once again taking up that noble challenge after what we can accurately call our "dark ages." The Aboriginal people of Canada have suffered through many decades of abominable and horrid oppression, often aimed at re-educating our young to make them less Native and more non-Native. Stories of Residential Schools, where the only thing learned was pain, are only recently coming to light. Today, we still live with those scars, and the healing continues. It's conferences like this, and people like you out there, that are helping to turn the circle of healing and education back onto its normal path.

The children that you will be facing have a long and noble ancestry, one deserving of the best future in the world. It's an awesome responsibility but it's not just your responsibility to lead these children. It's also up to the parents who raise these children to teach them that it's okay to be curious. It's also my obligation to teach, and others like me, in the writing that I do. It's everybody's duty out there, anyone that is a part of our society. As Chief Seattle is often quoted saying, "we are all strands in the web of life." The same goes for education. Everyday, if you're lucky, a dozen different people will tell you or show you something you didn't know when you woke up that morning. That too is education. And the amazing thing is, you people are gonna get paid to do this. Most of us have to do it for nothing.

But I am probably telling you things you already know. You must excuse me. I speak the obvious because it is often the easiest to overlook.

So here we all are, in the beautiful mountains of British Columbia, in the fabulous town of Whistler, discussing something so important to our people, something that we are all proud to be a part of, and more importantly, something we all love doing, in our own different ways. I try to educate through my writing. How many people here know that the word Ojibway, if translated properly, can mean one of three things? Pay attention, there's going to be an exam later. Ojibway is probably an Anishnawbe word, Anishnawbe being the more accurate name we call ourselves, meaning "the people." But the word Ojibway can be translated loosely as meaning "puckered." Doing some further investigation, I discovered that "puckered" could mean the special type of stitching we once used in our moccasins, or what human skin does when it burns. Yum.

There is also another school of thought that says that the word Ojibway is a bastardization of a Cree word meaning "those who stutter or do not speak our language properly." What a charming set of options.

Granted, that won't be on many college examinations, but as I said , each nugget of knowledge helps build that continent. As an Anishnawbe writer, having these little nuggets did "influence other thoughts" I had over the years, as stated in *Toronto at Dreamer's Rock*. And as a statement to those nasty old Crees, I try not to stutter.

With my writing, I try to educate not only the youth of our Nations, but also the adulthood. For, while we all may stop growing physically, Heaven help the person who stops growing mentally. I consider that true death. And there is so much out there to learn. I have promised myself that one of these days I will master my VCR. One of these days, I *will* read *Moby Dick*. One of these days, I *will* find out what the hell a "dangling participle" is. My mother didn't get her driver's license till she was somewhere around forty. You are never too old.

So, as a former student of the school system, and a continuous student of life, I would like to offer my humble thoughts on what I believe makes for a good educator and provides for a good education. Keep in mind that I do not have your training, your background, or your opportunity—I reason that getting paid to do this gives me sufficient credentials. And please remember that these are in no particular order.

1. Always try to be as interesting as the subject matter you are teaching. That is to say, I remember all too well far too many of my teachers looked and acted like they were going through the motions of teaching. A marked lack of enthusiasm from the teacher instilled much of the same attitude in me. I ended up just marking time in that class. As opposed to teachers who took an interest in the subject they

taught and the students they were teaching it too. I still recall animated teachers who infected me with a fervour towards certain subject matter. Sometimes one teacher's particular enthusiasm conflicted with another's and made for some interesting intellectual debates. For instance, a math teacher of mine once told our class that the great thing about math was that there was one, and only one answer. It was very cut and dry. Yet, an English teacher, that same year, told me the great thing about English, specifically analyzing books and literature, was that there was potential for more than one answer. I think that's why I always liked English better and became a playwright. It was multiple choice. It made life a little easier.

2. In this world dominated by the English or, in some places, the French language, and in a country where over ninety-five percent of the population is not Native, I would urge the important and continuous instruction of traditional Native materials. We as Native people are being continually bombarded by the more dominant culture and it is chipping away at our origins. Somebody once said that pretty soon pop culture will be our culture. I will even put a test out to the people in the audience. Who here can name all the castaways on *Gilligan's Island*? Yet, who can name the Chief or leader of his/her people at the time of contact? It's an ongoing dilemma that has to be, and finally is, being addressed. We are all affected by it. I, as a contemporary Ojibway storyteller, write specifically in English. I have to phone home to my Aunt on my Reserve when I need something translated into Ojibway for my plays. It is very awkward and embarrassing. I, myself, can only count up to eight in Ojibway. I think that says a lot. One way of addressing this issue is to show the underlying wisdom and of traditional ways and teachings. An example I would like to use is the Iroquois teaching of "the Three Sisters." When I first heard the term the Three Sisters, I immediately thought of the influential nineteenth-century Chekov play, *The Three Sisters*. But then again, as you may have heard, I'm a playwright—an Ojibway one. The Iroquois' Three Sisters refers to "Corn, Beans and Squash," staples of the Iroquois diet. During planting season, the three seeds are planted together for a variety of reasons. First of all, they all require different nutrients out of the ground so the danger of exhausting the soil is greatly lessened. Also, when growing, the squash remains on the ground, the corn reaches to the sky, and the

23

beans climb up the corn. A perfect, symbiotic relationship. And finally, when eaten all together, corn, beans and squash provide a complete protein, essential for life. Darn clever them Iroquois. They figured all this out without an Ojibway.

3. Don't be afraid to explore. In a recent play I've been working on, one of the characters is a Native science-fiction writer. As a result, I've incorporated an Aboriginal examination of the television series *Star Trek* and its philosophies. It was some of the most enjoyable and just downright-fun writing I have ever had the chance to do. Within that same play, I touch upon the similarities between the matriarchal storytelling societies of the Iroquois and Judaism. Exploring, in every way possible, can provide a special opportunity for the young to view their own culture through different and diverse eyes. While I am an incredibly strong proponent of strengthening our culture and protecting it at all costs, there is the potential of becoming myopic, which can be just as dangerous as losing the culture. One of the most memorable trips I made in my life was to New Zealand several years ago. *Aoterroa,* as the Indigenous Maori call it, the "Land of The Long White Cloud," provided me the opportunity to see another rich culture once dominated by a colonizing force, but now regaining much of what was lost. Sound familiar? The Maori now have guaranteed representation in the New Zealand Parliament, immersion schools, and a strong boat-building and carving tradition—something that the people in this province can appreciate. And, most important of all, they have learned that they can learn as much from other peoples of the world as they have to teach them. I guess I am what you might call a Maori wannabe.

4. Variety is the spice of life: to students; to teachers, I'm sure; to everyone. Practicality is another necessary ingredient in life. So, how to apply one to the other? Remembering back to my schooling days, those many, many years ago, I find myself recollecting some of the more interesting and unusual, and maybe non-traditional (in a non-Aboriginal context) uses of education. I remember once in an English class, having to write a review of a television show. I chose that old television classic, *The Incredible Hulk.* Before I had been just a non-discriminating adolescent watching an incredibly hokey show. But in doing the review, I had to watch the show objectively, trying to figure out what I liked and didn't like about it, and

then try and explain that on paper. I had to watch the show through different, critical eyes. As a result, I remember doing that review fondly. It sticks in my head. And that consisted of one single class during one year of my entire high school existence. It was different and fun. Another time I remember walking out onto a frozen lake and chopping ice from the lake to analyze for one of my classes. I remember thinking this is unusual and different. And I did it. I like reading and seeing Shakespeare as much as the next Native playwright, but seriously, what has he written lately? Unfortunately, the applications of sixteenth century Elizabethan English can sometimes stretch the concentration abilities of our Aboriginal youth—and many of the adults—to the limit. But Shakespeare, population density, trigonometry, looking at the innards of frogs, trying to play a trumpet, and learning how to shoot a basket—all regulation teaching fodder, and all important—are not *The Incredible Hulk*. Rumour has it he has a nasty temper.

So there you have it. Words and wisdom from somebody whose words and wisdom have been questioned many times. Take from my suggestions what you will. I'm getting paid regardless. But before we all go back up to our rooms and pack our dirty laundry for the trip home, I would like to leave you with a final thought.

Having never done a keynote address, I was a little nervous about what I should say, especially considering that I am not a professional educator and this is an education conference. I was told just to talk about myself, what I do, and how this may interrelate with the themes of the conference.

So I thought long and hard about what I do, how I do what I do, and how I got to be standing here in the wilds of Whistler. And the minor revelation that occurred to me, the epiphany of my life, is that I am no different from any other Native kid on any Reserve, or in any city for that matter. I'm not any brighter, cleverer, or even more gifted—I'm sorry to say—than anyone else. In fact, I'm quite average. Basically, the truth be told, I got to be an award-winning playwright, travel the world, meet interesting people in interesting places, do fun and fabulous things, and explore the wonderful world of education conferences because of the simple fact that I love to read. That's it.

Reading and imagination. Those are the keys to what I do. I

see it as a fundamental element to what everybody does, if they want to do it better. I am a good reader if I do say so myself. And by reading I don't just mean those classics of European literature covered in layers of dust. I mean everything: Stephen King, Thomas King, magazines, comic books, plays, legends, letters, and cereal boxes (that's where I learned that Cap'n Crunch wasn't a real Captain, it was just an honourary title, unlike Colonel Sanders). I will read anything that has an object, a noun, and a verb in the sentence. I'm not picky, I'll read anything. I'm what you might call a literary slut.

And now for the two words we've all been dying to hear today: in conclusion. It's been fun and a joy being here and talking with you all. I've learned a lot and added a few more islands to my still-growing continent. I hope I haven't bored you with my silly ramblings. Education is serious business, meaning it's to be taken seriously, but that doesn't mean we can't have some fun with it.
Thank you all and I wish you the best of luck. I just hope I won't be marked for grammar tonight.

And in my non-stuttering, non-stitching, non-burning language: *Meegwetch* and *co-obmen*.

# Sundances with Wolves

I have always wanted to say this, and for the first time in my life, I finally got to. About two months ago I was asked by some friends to hang out at a Powwow on Manitoulin Island with them.

Unfortunately I was unable to because, here it comes, "I had to fly to Hollywood to work on a script for Robert Redford's Sundance Institute." There, I said it again. I can now die a happy man.

I thought I could hear destiny calling my name when the Institute invited me to participate in the first-ever Native Screenwriters' Workshop. As one of three Canadians asked to attend, I jumped at the chance to visit the centre of the film universe and work on a project I had recently been formulating in my head. Simply put, it's an urban Native horror-comedy, and I thought this would be the perfect opportunity to put it in the metaphoric toaster and see what popped up.

It's no secret that Redford and the Institute have always been at the cutting edge of independent film development and promotion. The Sundance Film Festival is legendary. And the workshop was the latest endeavour to inject a more colourful—no pun intended—slice of life into the sometimes oblique Hollywood version of reality. So last month, we ten Aboriginal writers from across North America congregated at the UCLA campus, projects in hand, dreams in full force, ready to run our ideas up the, again metaphoric, flagpole and see who saluted them.

Projects and people ranged from a Yaqui-Mayan man who wants to turn his all-Native comic book into an animated movie, to a dark *X-Files*-type comedy by the Cheyenne director of the recent movie *Smoke Signals*. One older woman had taken seven years to write a wonderfully charming script about her mother, the first person to bring Christmas to the Navajo Reservation back in the 1950s.

27

It was truly a meeting of minds, Nations, and genres.

The ten-day workshop consisted of a series of meetings with two story editors, one Native, the other in a constant vain attempt to write the perfect screenplay. Key phrases in the process included "try and make the subtlety more obvious" and, my favourite, "sometimes it's possible to be a little too Indian." I may have a T-shirt printed with that message.

We were constantly subjected to various seminars and screenings meant to imprint upon us the value of independent film-making. Victor Nunez, Academy Award-nominated writer/director for *Ulee's Gold*, tried to impress upon us the value of not giving into the system and achieving your goals on your terms. Upon reflection, it sounds like every Native road-block I've ever heard about. Hmmmm, *Ulee's Roadblock*.

As for the big Kahuna himself (Bob, as we came to call him)... we, his loyal disciples, kept a candle burning, waiting for him to bless us with his presence. Though they would never admit it, I think he was probably the reason some of our humble writers came; to gaze lovingly on the Sundance Kid, the cowboy who never killed an Indian. But much like Samuel Beckett's play *Waiting for Godot*, he never showed up, though the promise hovered over our heads like the final number in a bingo game.

For the real filmmakers, there was another name associated with the workshop. He was on the Special Advisory Panel and, to many of us, he was as important as Redford, if not more so. And I had heard rumours that he was part Native, having actually lived a few years on an American Reservation as a child. But as a Canadian Aboriginal, I had long since become accustomed to hearing how everybody in the States was part Cherokee or Choctaw. The novelty had long since disappeared. But evidently it was true, he was part of us. Quentin Tarantino. The mere mention of his name was enough to make us filmmaker wannabes drool with anticipation. Alas, like Bob, he never showed up. Obviously he was busy in the same Beckett play.

Ten days passed. And in those ten days, much was learned and much was discussed. None of us got to do the amount of rewriting we all had anticipated. But we were in no position to be argumentative. We were in Hollywood, working with talented and successful people in a harsh and difficult industry. And we were all absolutely delighted that such a myopic industry was finally interested in hearing our stories, told our way. We were the first class. The inaugural Native Screenwriters' Workshop. We were told great things were expected of us. But we already knew that. We expect great things of ourselves. We consider ourselves contemporary storytellers. We're going from telling stories around the campfire to telling stories on the movie screen. Our vision quests include popcorn and a pop.

They say there are no new or original ideas left in Hollywood, but I'm not sure. I'm fairly certain I have the market cornered on urban Native horror-comedies.

One odd benefit from ten days in Los Angeles: I am now nineteen percent silicon. I'm trying to stay out of the sun for obvious reasons.

# Brother, It's Cold Outside

In case you haven't noticed, it's cold outside. And on these cold and chilly days, I find myself contemplating a cultural and historical curiosity, one that leaves me with a burning desire to ask my often equally frigid non-Native friends a question. The query goes something like, "Tell me again why your ancestors picked this country to move to?" A simple question. One I ask because *it's so cold outside*. I mean, being of Native descent myself, I *have* to live here. Several dozen millennia of freezing your buns off sort of make you attached to the place. But I will admit, being half white makes staying warm in this environment a little more difficult.

So to all the non-Native people shivering around their televisions at this very moment, I ask you once more: Why did your people come here voluntarily? *It's cold here.* Or didn't your ancestors read that in the pamphlets? And this is only Toronto. I won't even bother discussing the distinctive winter weather of Regina or Winnipeg.

Now being somewhat of a history buff, I understand the whole "seeking to escape oppression" concept. We Native people have faced a little oppression ourselves in our history but you don't see us running to one of the coldest countries in the world to try and improve our lives. Of all the countries in this big old world, why pick The Great White North (no ethnic pun intended)? I know Tourism Canada is gonna kill me, but need I remind you, *it's cold here!* Couldn't the white folk have planted potatoes in Florida? There were a lot of wide, open spaces in the Bahamas. There were railways being built in Venezuela and lots of places in St. Lucia in which to hide from despots and dictators. *It's not cold there!*

Now trust me, this isn't some anti-immigration rant, it's an anti-frostbite one. I mean, I practically live in Thai restaurants, have a fondness for Italian leather, and have several Mexican quilts on my bed to keep me warm on these cold, cold nights. Now think about it. What's the common denominator of all these countries? They're warm. *And it's cold here.*

To me, it's just a question of sheer logic, like, "Tell me again? Why did you vote for the Tories?"

# Some Don't Like It Hot

Toronto is a very large and prosperous city. The largest in Canada in fact. And I've always prided myself on telling people from across Canada and around the world how metropolitan Toronto is and the fact that if you need something, anything, chances are you can find it somewhere with in the city boundaries. Evidently I was in error. In this city of almost three million people, it is virtually impossible to get a small air conditioner. Anywhere. I know because I worked up quite a sweat trying to locate one.

My girlfriend and I have just bought a house and are currently renovating it. For one reason or another, the new bedroom is substantially hotter than the one we're leaving. The logical conclusion was made and I went in search of an air conditioner, one small enough to fit vertically in the only window available. About five or six thousand B.T.U. (what ever the hell those are) would be just about right. Anything higher would trip a breaker switch.

My first stop, Home Depot. They only had 10,000 B.T.U. machines. Same with Canadian Tire. Then I journeyed to the Toronto landmark known as Honest Ed's, the famous bargain place. The only air conditioner they had cost about a $1,000. I could get a plane ticket to the Arctic for that amount of money. Eatons doesn't carry them anymore and the venerable Hudson's Bay Company had only one left in the store, and it was way too big for my needs. I'm running out of alternatives as well as clothes not soaked in sweat.

In this consumer driven society, I am having some difficulty figuring out why a simple small air conditioner is so close to extinction. About ten years ago, I bought an air conditioner. That one too was difficult to locate because I bought it during the first heat wave of the summer, when appliance stores were flooded with patrons eager to avoid the summer heat and roll around naked in cool ecstasy. That I could understand. But here we are, near the tail end of

July, and a good air conditioner is still difficult to locate. It doesn't make sense. There's only probably a few more weeks of really hot weather left so there can't be that big a run on them.

But now I am quite tempted to start a company that manufactures these things because I can't be the only person out there on a mission like this. I know there's a market out there. You would think the existing manufacturers of these mechanisms would plan ahead. This is Canada. A nation of people who love the cold. Maybe love isn't the word. A nation of people who are conditioned (pun intended) to the cold. I personally think air conditioning, next to fire and the wheel, is one of the three greatest inventions ever created.

So now it seems I must move into our new house disheartened. Disheartened and hot. Not a good combination for your first home. I know somewhere out there, is a small air conditioner with my name on it. I can here it calling my name across the sweltering landscape. Maybe I'll have to make one of those clandestine trips across the border the provincial and federal governments discourage.

But what really gets me, is the alternative reality of the situation. Believe it or not, it is probably easier, in our beloved city of Toronto, to get crack cocaine, kiddy porn, and probably a gun, then a small 6,000 B.T.U. air conditioner.

Welcome to Toronto.

# Two Sides of the Coin

Davis Inlet. Mention that name and dark, depressing images immediately come to mind. At least they did to me when I learned I'd be making a day trip to this infamous community. I envisioned scenes of poverty, anarchy, and substance abuse, just to name a few. You remember Davis Inlet. That's the community of people that was forcibly relocated thirty years ago. These people ended up on some small island in the middle of nowhere, put there by the government for some obscure bureaucratic reason. And didn't they do that same thing to an Inuit community back in the 1950s; bundle them all up and ship them from northern Quebec to an island in the far, far north, to an area they were not familiar with? All in the name of furthering Canada's claim to the Arctic Archipelago by populating it with people. Much like Davis Inlet, these people are saying "enough is enough." They want to go back home and are petitioning the government for compensation.

Putting it in a different context, it's like saying, let's put everybody in Sudbury on some island in the middle of James Bay and see how they survive. But it seems to me that the government doesn't do things like that to non-Native communities. Why am I not surprised?

So I came to this community on the stunningly beautiful shores of Labrador and saw some of the things I expected to see. Many of the walls in Davis Inlet are covered in graffiti, including some disgusting suggestions on the door of a Nun's home in the community. I noticed most of the public buildings no longer have glass windows. Instead, it's more logical to use a form of unbreakable plastic. The entrance to the school I visited looked like a bunker under siege: dark, decorated with heavy mesh screening, ominous looking, and heavily fortified. I admit it, I felt sorry for this community.

But there were other things I saw in this windswept, frozen

village, things that I had not been expecting that made me realize this community had been getting a bum rap. For instance, I have never been to a place where the children are so quick to smile. Walking down the hallways of the school these kids would come up to me with a big smile and boldly ask, "Hi, what's your name?"

At the airport—a postage-stamp-sized, flat piece of snow-covered land—I watched four young kids, all younger than seven, running around the building and through the office in glorious celebration of anarchy. They climbed on everything, played everywhere, and they were having fun. Not just average fun, but the kind of fun that comes with complete freedom. The parents were busy working, processing the half-dozen or so passengers in a cold aluminum room, completely oblivious to the chaos their kids were creating and enjoying. These were happy kids.

And in the same school that I described as a bunker, the students were rehearsing a play they had written and were performing for the community. It was a play about solvent abuse, specifically gas sniffing, and how it's often cyclical; the parents drink, so the kids think it's okay to do similar stuff. And the play was completely in Innu, the students' Native language. Even though I had only been in Davis Inlet for a few hours, I felt proud of these students.

During the skidoo trip back to the airport, I looked over at the setting sun, and back at my very brief encounter with this community. Thoughts were running through my head. We passed a tame wolf that lived in the town, a beautiful animal with a glorious winter coat that a family had adopted. I saw the new houses being put in. And then the skidoo blew up. Or more correctly, the voltage regulator shorted out and smoke started pouring from the engine. On the walk up to the airport, in the increasingly frigid twilight, I had more time to reflect.

It will be at least another five or six years before the new village the government is building for this community is ready for occupancy. And these kids will be young adults by then. There is hope for Davis Inlet.

# LISTOMANIA
## (THE BOOK OF LISTS)

## You Know You're Old When...

As winter slowly turns into spring, and the continuous cycle of the seasons completes another full year, it occurs to you that yet another birthday is soon approaching. And you have mixed feelings about it. In your early years, you measured birthdays by different milestones.

For instance, you turn thirteen, and you are officially a teenager (parents be afraid, be very afraid). You turn sixteen, and you can get a driver's license (other drivers be afraid, very afraid). You turn nineteen, and you are legal for just about everything. And conversely, you are also responsible for everything you do. You turn twenty-five, and you are no longer eligible for youth-oriented job-employment programs—the first kink in your imaginary armour of agelessness. You crest the hill known as thirty, and well... this is a particularly difficult birthday because you now begin to realize that you're getting ever so slightly older. At age thirty-three Christ and Crazy Horse died. You wonder: what have you done with your life?

And from here, the years and pounds begin to add up a little too quickly and comfortably. And it's your turn to be afraid, very afraid.

Our culture and teachings have taught us to revere and respect our Elders. Growing old is part of the cycle of life, like the seasons. I have trouble benignly remembering that fact when it takes at least two days to recover from pushing a car out of a snowdrift. And it was a small car. And it wasn't a particularly deep snowdrift.

Recently I have begun to notice various uncomfortable signs that "the times they are a changin'" (for those old enough to remember that song), and they're a changin' none too easily. In my own life, I've observed numerous signs from the Creator gently reminding me that I am not a young man anymore. At the age of thirty-six, soon to be thirty-seven, I am a little over halfway past the life expectancy of a Canadian Aboriginal male. Evidently, physically speaking, it's downhill from here. The Elder years are fast approaching. Well, maybe someone will carry my luggage from now on and people will actually listen to what I have to say.

I have taken the liberty of recording some of those "gentle reminders" for your interest. Feel free to add your own reminders, or just cry along with me. The choice is yours.

You know you're old when:

You realize the Zorro T-shirt you put on might not be appropriate for somebody your age. You begin looking for beer and sport T-shirts favoured by your uncles. If you're lucky, you might be able to find that prized golf or fishing shirt. Welcome to the club. You now dress like your uncles.

You are at the dentist, and as the dental hygienist is cleaning your teeth, she comments casually that she saw one of your plays when she was in high school. "But I don't remember which one it was. That was so long ago." You refrain from responding as your heart cries out because, at that moment, she has several sharp implements deep inside your mouth. You decide to overlook it this time.

Every time you put on a sweater, your girlfriend can automatically tell which decade you bought it in. Nobody told me velour was out!

Your girlfriend steals all your batteries for her own personal reasons and refuses to tell you why. And you don't care.

You find out fifty percent of the Native population is under twenty-five. You do the math and realize you have underwear that is older than half the Aboriginal community.

And scariest of all, your mother makes sense.

And this was just today!

## Ask Me No Stupid Questions and I'll Tell You No Lies

Recently I was longingly and wistfully looking at some photographs I took several years ago, during a fantastic and amazing trip to the South Pacific. I had managed to stick my big toe in the surf in Fiji, Hawaii, and, most fabulous of all, New Zealand, where I was lucky enough to frolic with the Maori (now there's a mental image for you).

And while there, me and a friend found ourselves attending a Maori play in a theatre located down by the waterfront in Auckland. A fellow theatre patron caught my eye because he looked exceedingly familiar to me. One of those faces that looks like you should know it but you can't put your finger on why or where. It bugged me during the entire show, until afterwards when my friend and I were invited to share a drink with the cast and crew. It was there that I was introduced to this somewhat familiar face.

It turns out that he was the lead singer from the rock group Fine Young Cannibals, and he was on some sort of personal odyssey, travelling through New Zealand and, as luck would have it, decided to include this Maori play on his agenda. So here I am, in New Zealand, talking with a Black British rock star, and the first question he asks me is "so, what's it like being Indian in Canada?"

You travel the world, and no matter where you go, or whom you meet, you always get asked silly and bizarre questions. It never seems to end. Now in all fairness to my Fine Young Cannibal friend, he was a very gracious and intelligent man and I bear him no grudge. But, as a Native person, the constant barrage of questions that I, and I'm sure other Native people, have to face—ones that could be answered by the questioners themselves with just a little bit of common sense if they thought about it, *Goddamn it*—is becoming tiresome.

Back when I used to be the Artistic Director of Native Earth Performing Arts, our office was frequently flooded with these ques-

41

tionable inquiries. In fact, we all lived in fear of hearing the dreaded cry from whoever answered the phones: "it's one of those calls!"

For instance: *"I'm calling to find out if you do any cere- monies, and can we hire you to come out and do some? If not, do you know of any books that we could get them from?"*

Questions like this are borderline insulting. I'm surprised some entrepreneurial hotshot hasn't already come up with a "Ceremonies 'R' Us" kind of organization. I also hear some people are charging for the experience of sweating in a "genuine" sweat lodge. How do these capitalists come up with the proper price? Do you get charged per pint of sweat or by the amount of spiritual com- fort you find?

*"I'm wondering if I can send you my play. I'd like you to con- sider producing it at your theatre. No, I'm not Native, but because my play has to do with mythology, Celtic mythology to be specific, and I know a lot of Native plays have to do with mythology, I thought there might be some sort of bond or connection there. After all, mythology is universal. Don't you think?"*

No I don't.

*"Do you know where I can get my hands on some authentic Native clothing?"*

It depends on what you call "authentic." Providing these peo- ple aren't talking about buckskin or blankets, I don't know what to tell them. I have two Dorothy Grant shirts. She's a fabulous Haida clothing designer from the West Coast, and she incorporates Haida art and mythology into her clothing. Yet the label on the shirt states "made in Hong Kong." Unless Hong Kong is a Reserve I don't know about, what is "authentic Native clothing?"

*"I was wondering if you might be able to help me. I'm with a tour company and we're trying to locate a Native Elder to come in and visit with some tourists from Germany. He doesn't have to do anything, just visit and talk with them. Let them get to know him. It would be even better if he could be dressed traditionally."*

I'm sure it would be. Most of the Elders I know wear work- boots, jeans or workpants, maybe a plaid shirt, sometimes a baseball cap, and usually glasses. Sure, I can get you one of those. Do you want him with or without the package of cigarettes?

You get questions like this and you find yourself weighing

42

the pros and cons of the situation. Do I want to trouble somebody I know and respect and make him or her available for display, putting him/her in the position to be "oohhed" and "aaahhhed" over? Or do I ignore the call, even though companies like this usually have some money to pay, money that would, no doubt, help in these economically depressed times?

That's the problem with stupid questions. If you look at them from a dozen different angles, one or two of those angles might produce a question that, when answered, might actually offer an opportunity to do Native people some good. It's called a conundrum.

Final note: On the flight home from New Zealand, we saw David Bowie and his wife Iman on our plane, but they didn't ask us anything.

# The First Annual Aboriginal Trivia Contest

Think you know everything there is to know about being Native/Aboriginal/Indigenous/First Nations/Indian (better known as a NAIFNI)? Or maybe you know somebody who's an annoying know-it-all? What better way to start off the year than putting yourself and your friends to the test. After all, it's better to know you're a know-it-all than to just think you're a know-it-all! It's better than nothing at all.

If you score twelve or more, then you get an "A" for "Aboriginal Effort." Ten or more, "B" for "Better than average." If you score an eight or more, than you get a "C" for "Could do better, but better than most." Four or more gets you a "D" for "Do more work." Anything less gets you an "E" for "Education" (as in "the need for more...")

Easy:

1. What was the original name for the Assembly of First Nations before it was changed back in the early 80s?

2. What was the name of the Native actor who played Jesse Jim on that Canadian television classic, *The Beachcombers*?

3. What Native Language is the word "Canada" derived from?

4. The Northwest Territories will be divided into two separate regions. One is called Nunavut. What will be the name of the other territory?

5. In what province were the Beothuk Indians exterminated in the 1800s?

Moderate:

1. In what fictional community do Tomson Highway's *The Rez Sisters* and *Dry Lips Oughta Move To Kapuskasing* occur?

2. What was the name of the "Indian" character in that other classic Canadian television show, *The Forest Rangers*?

3. Which of these Nations is not one of the Dene: the Dogrib, Slavey, Chipawyan, or Carrier?

4. What year was Louis Riel hung for treason?

5. What year was Bill C-31 officially passed by Canada's Parliament?

Difficult:

1. In reference to the answer of question one, who was responsible for establishing that organization way back in 1967?

2. What was the name given to the Indigenous people by the Vikings when they first landed in Atlantic Canada a thousand years ago?

3. What does the word "Kashtin" actually mean?

4. What was the name of the "Indian" in the disco group, The Village People?

5. What well-known American tribe has a language exceedingly similar to the Dene's?

Answers:

Easy:
1. National Indian Brotherhood
2. Pat John
3. Iroquoian
4. North West Territories
5. Newfoundland

45

Moderate:
1. Wasaychigan Hill
2. Joe Two Rivers
3. Carrier
4. 1885
5. 1985

Difficult:
1. George Manuel
2. Skraelings
3. Tornado
4. Felipe
5. The Navajo (who call themselves the Dine)

# The Seven "C's" of Canadian Colonization

On June 24, 1997, all of Newfoundland celebrated the five hundredth anniversary of the landing of John Cabot's ship, the *Matthew*, on the island. Back in 1597, Cabot's was the first European ship to visit Canada (not including the Viking's short stay in Canada's tenth province, back around 1000 A.D.). A fabulous party was held, including a cameo appearance from her Majesty, the Queen herself.

But not all were happy with the planned festivities. The Assembly of First Nations, as well as many other Native organizations and individuals, didn't really see this as something to celebrate. Some consider Cabot's arrival as the beginning of a campaign of genocide and cultural destruction that has lasted five hundred years. As an example, less than three centuries after Cabot's landfall, the Beothuks, Newfoundland's Indigenous people, were extinct. And while that blame can't be laid directly on Cabot's shoulders, most Natives believe it started with him. At least in Canada.

But Cabot had a lot of company. History has shown that many European explorers laid the foundation for the colonization of our little country. Other explorers of the unknown have had effects on Canada and its native people. And a surprising and interesting fact is that the names of many of these explorers start with the letter "C." Perhaps this is the prerequisite for conquering Canada. For instance:

*Columbus:* The man who made getting lost an art form. He is the prototype of men refusing to believe they are lost and ask for directions. While not specifically or directly connected to Canada, his arrival in the Bahamas can be viewed as one earthquake starting several tidal waves. It is ironic that many white people every year still like to "discover" the Bahamas, and other spots in the Caribbean and Mexico that he came upon. Perhaps white people are migratory.

*Cortez:* Again, while not directly related to Canada, his actions have had wide-reaching effects. He conquered an empire (the Aztecs) and was actually one of the few Conquistadors to die a rich man. At one point, he took a Native woman as a mistress and Christianized her to make her more acceptable. Known for his ambition, womanizing, and twice being arrested for breach of trust, it's no wonder that he was a politician—a mayor in a town in Cuba.

*Cabot:* Cabot's real name was Giovanni Caboto. Probably the first of many men to change his name to get into Canada. He was amazed by the number of fish available offshore. It is rumoured the crew attached ropes to baskets to lower them into the water, and pulled them up overflowing with fish. Ahh, the memories. The first case of foreigners plundering the Grand Banks.

*Cartier:* Founder of Quebec City in 1534. Misunderstood what the local Natives were saying when he asked them "what do you call this land?" as he indicated the countryside with his hand. Unfortunately the Native people looked where he was actually pointing, at their village, and replied, "Kanata: a group of huts or a village." Kanata is now Canada. The first misunderstanding between the French and Native population. Not the last.

*Champlain:* The explorer of much of Central Canada. Though he spent decades in the New World, Champlain never, oddly enough, bothered to learn any of the aboriginal languages of the people he worked with and exploited. Even then, Quebec's Language Bill 101 was in effect.

*Cook:* Explored much of the coast of British Columbia after discovering Tahiti and the Hawaiian islands while looking for the Northwest Passage. His first claim to fame was his meticulous charting of the St. Lawrence River—in preparation for the British assault on the French at Quebec. He is also known for his precise charting of the whole length of the rugged coast of Newfoundland. One of the first cases of Easterners moving to the West Coast.

*Christ:* Subject of the world's first and bestselling "biography."

48

Christ did more to change the lives of Canada's Indigenous people than all the explorers put together. Unfortunately, this change was usually for the worst: think of the Jesuits and, more recently, the Residential Schools. But many have embraced the teachings of this man and found happiness. The Church brought more than just Christ's messages to the Native people, it also brought bingo.

Other honourable mentions of people "discovering and conquering" this continent whose names begin with the letter "C": Clark (of Lewis and Clark fame), who went to the Pacific Northwest looking for dinosaurs, and Custer, every Aboriginal's favourite example of "do onto others as you would have them do unto you." But they lack that specific Canadian connection.

Most of these men were crawling through Canada's coast and interior looking for gold, jewels, and spices, or, more specifically, a new trade route to India or China. On June 24th, 1997, I thought it would be ironic and fitting for there to be a whole line of Native protesters waiting on shore for the landing of the *Matthew*, all holding signs saying "India and China: That Way," pointing north to the Northwest Passage. It would have done more to honour the spirit of these explorers than what the people in Newfoundland had planned.

Or, better yet, they should have had some Chinese or South Asians waiting on shore. That would have thrown them for a loop.

# A Lexicon of Aboriginal Trivia, from A to Z

With the growing interest in all things Native, a few small but interesting details of everyday (or not so everyday) Aboriginal life sometime fall through the cracks. The following are tidbits of trivia for the reader to do with what he or she pleases.

*Apache:* In the movie *Rambo II*, Sylvester Stallone's killing-machine character is reported as being half German and half Apache. One government agent in the film sums it up by saying "God, what a mix!"

*Break a leg:* In reference to the two famous confrontations that happened in Wounded Knee, South Dakota, Native actors, hoping for a good show, use the term "Wounded Knee" instead of "break a leg."

*Crum:* George Crum, a Native cook working at the Saratoga Springs Resort in New York, accidentally invented the potato chip in 1853. When a customer complained that the fried potato wedges he was served were too big and not salty enough, Crum retaliated by serving the gentleman wafer-thin potato slices covered in salt—as a joke. Evidently the joke took off.

*Dartmouth:* This top-notch American ivy league university located in New Hampshire originally started out as a seminary for educating American Indians. An institute for redskins instead of bluebloods.

*Education:* Having an MBA now stands for having Mixed Blood Ancestry. Or Me Big Aboriginal.

*F.B.I.:* Amongst Native Nations in America, F.B.I. stands for Full Blooded Indian, while in Canada, DIA (Department of Indian

Affairs) now stands for those "Damn Indian Agents."

*Grey Owl:* While known as a famous Aboriginal imposter, this Englishman claimed to actually be half Jacarilla Apache, not Ojibway or Cree as Canadian mythology would suggest. He may even be related to Rambo.

*Hui Shun:* A Chinese Buddhist priest and explorer who also supposedly "discovered" America in 458 A.D. and tried to convert local Indians to Buddhism. Allegedly he named Guatemala in honour of Gautama Buddha.

*Indian Summer:* The politically correct now refer to this time of fall as "First Nations Summer." I kid you not.

*Jobs:* Though Native people in the United States make up less than one percent of the overall population, they are estimated to make up over ten percent (a lot of them Iroquois) of the high iron workforce, building skyscrapers, bridges, and the like.

*Kemosaabe: Kemosaabe* is an actual word in the Ojibway language. It means "to peek or look through," i.e., a mask. A liberal translation might also include a "peeping Tom."

*Little Bighorn:* The only non-Native survivor of Custer's Seventh Cavalry was a horse ironically named Commanche, ridden by a Captain Keogh. The horse suffered seven wounds, three of them serious. Treated as a war hero, the horse lived till 1893 when it died at the age of thirty.

*May, Karl:* One of Hitler's favourite authors was Karl May, who wrote a series of books at the turn of the century romanticizing the American Indian in the old West. May's books are still in print and popular in Germany. Many people believe them to be the root of the German preoccupation with Native people.

*Names:* Pocahontas was not her real name. It was actually a nickname given to her by her father meaning "playful one." Her real

51

name was actually Matoaka.

*Ouch:* The translation of this word varies from community to community. In Curve Lake you would say "owe-ee," where as on Manitoulin Island the pronunciation would be "eye-yow," and in at least one Reserve in Southwestern Ontario it would be "eee-yow." The Tyendinaga use the term "agee" and claim that the term hockey is derived from it; when White people saw Mohawks being slammed against the boards, they would cry out "agee" in pain. Agee/hockey... think about it.

*Pool:* These days, in playing the game of pool, after sinking the first ball, instead of calling stripes/highball, or colours/lowball, trendy Natives call "halfbreeds or fullbloods."

*Quipu:* Elaborately knotted strings with which the Incas recorded virtually every important aspect of their civilization. The position and number of knots on each individual string had a precise meaning. It was their form of writing and accounting.

*Recreational Vehicles:* The Winnebago Nation, located along the shores of Lake Superior, has officially changed its name to Hocak Wyijaci. Put that on a RV.

*Saugeen:* A Native Reserve in Ontario that is investigating the possibility of unionizing the Band Office, a first in First Nations. Saugeen Local 001. Only problem: who would care if the Band Office went on strike?

*Tonto:* The actor who played Tonto was actually from the Six Nations Reserve near Brantford, Ontario. Jay Silverheels was his professional name; his real name was actually Harry Smith. Perhaps a distant relation to Pocahontas' John Smith?

*Ukrainians:* There seems to be a bizarre artistic connection between Ukrainians and Native people. Note author W.P. Kinsella, playwright George Ryga, and actor Michael Zenon. Zenon is, no doubt, familiar to millions of older Canadians as Joe Two Rivers from the ancient television series, *The Forest Rangers.*

*Vegetables:* Native contributions to international cuisine include the potato and the tomato. So the Irish and the Italians owe us an amazing debt of gratitude.

*Wannabes:* People who "wannabe" Indian. Not to be confused with "should-a-beens," people who are not Native but for one reason or another, should have been.

*Xinxa:* A fictional tribe of Indians from Guatemala that gave Lamont Cranston, otherwise know as the pulp and movie hero "The Shadow," a fire opal ring to assist him in fighting crime. "Who knows what tribes lurk in the heart of Guatemala? The Shadow knows!"

*Yuchi:* An Aboriginal nation that was moved from Georgia to Oklahoma in 1836, and is believed to be, by some authorities, one of the "Lost Tribes of Israel." As recently as 1975, *Newsweek* said that "some specialists in American folklore think the customs, language and appearance of the Yuchi... imply an old Jewish heritage." Oy!

*Zero:* The Mayan base twenty-number system, which included zero, had been developed a thousand years in advance of its use elsewhere, and Mayan astronomers were capable of astonishing precision in charting the heavens.

# The Reserves are Alive with the Sound of Music

Several nights ago I was over at the home of a couple of associates, throwing back a few beers and discussing a potential business project we were all interested in. It was one of those concepts that, if pulled off properly, could be quite fun and even make history. But done wrong... well, let's just say it could blow up in our hands, causing us a lot of embarrassment and, no doubt, a lot of money. But we also made the startling discovery that the more beer you drink, the rosier and more optimistic things appear. I doubt if we were the first to discover that.

So, basically, my friends wanted to know if I'd be interested in writing a Native musical with them. You know, with singing Indians, broad emotions, and a dance number to beat all hell! I had visions of rows and rows of dancing Aboriginals, scantily clad, kicking their feet up in synchronous rhythm as they danced to the beat of a traditional orchestra. The kind of show that would have flying feathers and fluff, for sure. Now the thing is, I don't know if that image excites or scares me!

Now, other than the fact that I don't write or read music—I don't even own a stereo, for that matter—I thought this could be fun.

It wasn't long before all the little wheels in my head began turning. After several centuries of cultural appropriation, I was in a position to turn the proverbial tables on the appropriators. I immediately started thinking of potentially viable Native interpretations of very successful and popular musicals already in existence—ones I could raid... oops, I mean liberate... and give a good and cultured home on some far-off Reserve.

For instance, a few of my favourites are:

*Phantom of the Bingo Hall:* the charming story of a demented and disfigured bingo caller.

*Showcanoe:* a period piece about when Native people canoed across the Great Lakes in search of great blueberries.

*Jesus Christ Superchief:* Jesus Christ arrives on an Ontario Reserve only to find people fight there more than in the Middle East.

*Ever Crazy for You:* A Vegas-type musical with scantily clad girls (I told you!) done Aboriginal style, taking place in Casino Rama. The reason the girls are scantily clad: they lost their shirts.

*Oka-lahoma (Where the Wind Goes Whistling Through the Pines):* Fun, laughter and romance with the S.Q. (Quebec's provincial police force) at the barricades.

*West Bay Story:* The riveting story of love amidst opposing clans fighting it out on Manitoulin Island.

*Elijah:* The political-biography musical of a powerful man, featuring the hit song "Don't Cry For Me, Manitoba."

*Skirmish Line:* Picture a "chorus-line" of Warriors at Oka, all in fatigues, kicking up a fuss.

*Miss Sagamok:* A giant canoe floats down to the floor from the ceiling to save all the inhabitants.

Other potential Aboriginal adaptations include *Joseph and the Amazing Technicolour Ribbonshirt*, *Mii-Da* (an Ojibway word meaning animal fat or "grease"), and *H.M.S. Chichiman*. I know the possibilities are endless but... I don't know, they all sound kind of hokey. Although, essentially, most musicals are.

Of course, I could try adapting something from another medium for the musical stage. How about *Dances With Wolves* as a musical? Then again, I doubt all the buffalo would fit on stage for the stampede. Besides, I don't think the stagehands have it in their contracts to clean up after buffalo.

# The Behind-the-Scenes Awards

I write this as I am travelling home on a plane, exhausted and delighted, after attending yet another fine film festival—my fourth journey in a row for this particular festival. No, I'm not returning from Cannes (no tan and certainly no scantily clad girls, although I do have a suggestion for the festival organizers for next year...), nor the Toronto International (since I live in Toronto it would be kind of hard to fly home from it), nor Sundance (no Robert Redford in sight and certainly no mountains).

I am, of course, referring to the Dreamspeakers Aboriginal Film Festival, held annually in Edmonton. It's the kind of place where novice writers, directors and actors rub elbows and eat breakfast with practically the whole cast of *North of Sixty*, along with Graham Greene, Gary Farmer, and quite a few other notable Natives.

And the reason these people are here, other than to do that elbow rubbing thing I mentioned earlier, is to attend the inaugural presentation of the first annual Aboriginal Film Awards, affectionately known as the "Abies."

Hosted by the dapper, charming, and remarkably tall Tom Jackson, these awards celebrate the best of Aboriginal film and video. Awards for "best production," "best acting," and "best documentary" were handed out to deserving winners, and there was a special retrospective salute to the career of Graham Greene.

But as an invited delegate privy to the behind-the-scenes dramas that were constantly unfolding backstage during the awards ceremony, as well as the whole festival itself, I couldn't help but feel that perhaps a few awards were being left out. There should be some special awards for the people involved in the festival itself, as well as in the audience.

So, in the spirit of the First Annual "Abie" awards, may I present the first annual Behind-the-Scenes Dreamspeakers Awards or the "BTSDAs" (pronounced just the way it's spelled).

*Best Original Request by a Visiting Group (Entertainment Category):* The award goes to the Aztec Fire Dancers that phoned Dreamspeakers' organizers to ask if they could find the dancers a large snake for their act.

*Best-Kept Sudden Realization/Concern:* The award goes to the Dreamspeakers staff that suddenly realized during the packed gala dinner and entertainment show that the Aztec Fire Dancers were using real fire and producing lots of smoke in a room full of very well-dressed and elegant people, as well as lots and lots of smoke detectors and sprinklers.

*Best Spontaneous Musical Incident:* The award goes to the jam session between the Billy Joe Green Band, Gary Farmer (harmonica), and Pura Fe (vocals).

*Best Pick-up Line:* The Award goes to the unnamed gentleman who used the line "Hey, wanna go up to my room and do a little throat singing?"

*Most Annoying and Often Repeated Question:* The award goes to all the people who posed the same question to the Maori delegation, visiting all the way from New Zealand: "What's your opinion of the movie *Once Were Warriors*"?

*Best Instance of a Subject Not Discussed by Two Adults Over Dinner:* The award goes to Jordan Wheeler, story editor for *North of Sixty*, and Drew Hayden Taylor, disgruntled critic.

*Best Response to Compliment:* The award goes the gentleman who was told he had a "nice butt." His response: "I can pick quarters up off the ground with it."

*Most Questionable/Dubious Visual Image:* The award goes to anyone actually visualizing this guy picking quarters up with his butt!

57

*Most Interesting and Revealing Detail Missed by Most People:* The award goes to whoever noticed that on the list of award nominations handed out at the gala dinner, the first nominee in each category was always the winner, due to a printing oversight.

*Worst Mistake by an Ojibway Writer:* The award goes to yours' truly for accepting an offer to play "an innocent little game" of pool with Gary Farmer.

# Reasons Why You Should Be Nice to Native People

In this era of unsettled land claims, government cutbacks, and the continuing unacceptable levels of unemployment and mortality, it's no wonder Native people across Canada are sometimes viewed as, shall we say, pissed off at the world. And those are just a few of the many larger issues that happen to make the evening papers. On a smaller level, a more personal and everyday kind of existence, the complaints and irritants continue.

I refer to the minor annoyances that make living as an Aboriginal person in Canada less than enjoyable. So, since the education of those who just don't know what life is like as an Aboriginal person in Canada is always half the battle, I humbly present six minor irritations in the everyday life of a Canadian Native person for your consideration.

1. Non-Native people who try to "out-Indian" Native people. Ever sit in a sweat lodge of an approximate temperature of sixty to eighty degrees Celsius with a non-Native person that is reciting an incredibly long prayer thanking the Grandmothers, the Grandfathers, and everybody else who could possibly be listening up there, as various parts of that non-Native's anatomy shrivel up and fall off from the heat?

2. The fact that it is rapidly becoming unsafe to wear traditional clothing made of buckskin or fur because of spray paint-wielding lunatics on a mission to destroy thousands of years of heritage. Why can't they destroy something really horrible, like polyester?

3. People called New Agers who chase Native people around because they think there's a spiritual connection there somewhere. If I see one more New Ager approach me at a Powwow or a conference, shoving those damn crystals at me, I hereby refuse to be responsible for my actions or where those crystals may end up anatomically.

4. The fact that it's customary for Native people to expect

59

everything they do or every decision they make to have repercussions seven generations down the road. And how amazingly true that's become concerning the settling of land claims in this country. We'll be lucky if they get settled by our tenth generation. Looking on the bright side, at least it's job security for treaty researchers, lawyers and politicians.

5. The fact that the Native people of this country are constantly being referred to as "Canada's Tragedy," "The Dispossessed," or "The Sad and Unfortunate Story of Canada's Native People." It's always something depressing like that. And if you're always called names like this, pretty soon you'll start to believe it. I refuse to be tragic, or sad, or depressed; there's too much to be delighted with in our cultures. Someday I want to see headlines like "Those Happy People of Manitoulin Island" or "Those Laugh-a-Minute Crees in Northern Alberta."

6. The millions upon millions of people you meet in bars, airplanes, classrooms, libraries, etc., who say "I've got some Indian blood in me too." If every Native person I know gave the government a nickel for every non-Native person who has claimed this, the national debt would vanish with money left over to reinstate all the funding cut to Native programs. I once knew a girl in high school who told me that she had a drop of Native blood in her. "A long time ago, my Great Grandmother was raped by a Mohawk." Now there's a proud lineage.

7. All the stupid questions we get asked. Like, "Can you ride a horse?" Or, "What's it like living on a Reserve?" "Do you know Graham Greene?" "What did you think of *Dances With Wolves*?" "Last week I had a dream about a plaid horse and a talking feather. What does it mean?" Perhaps that you should get help.

# A HORSE OF A DIFFERENT COLOUR
## (PROS AND CONS OF BEING WHO YOU ARE)

# What to Believe?

Every once in a while, something happens in most people's lives that makes them wonder about what they believe, what they don't believe, what they should believe, and what they're afraid to believe. Oddly enough, my believability dilemma originated from something as obscure as the new *Tarzan and the Lost City* movie, if you can believe it.

In this rather mediocre film, Tarzan, the all-powerful White demi-god, races through the jungle trying to save the local Indigenous people and the lost city of Opar from some vicious and greedy white men that are a combination of explorers, archaeologists, and so-called representatives of civilization. How many times have we heard that before? After getting over the obvious cultural déjà vu, several sequences within the movie made me laugh in my seat and shake my head in artistic disbelief.

Assisting Tarzan in his noble quest is the chief of the local tribe, who also happens to be the tribal shaman/medicine man in possession of some very interesting powers. He has the ability to suddenly appear out of nowhere as a swarm of bees that covers the unconscious cobra-bitten Tarzan, hiding him from the evil White people. At various other times in the movie, after saving Tarzan from the cobra venom with a single touch, this same man turns himself into a giant cobra (evidently there are a lot of cobras in Africa). He is also impervious to bullets; they just pass through him with barely a ripple. And he creates entire living warriors out of a single one-inch bone fragment.

Putting aside the basic assumption that a tribe with such a bag of cool tricks up its sleeve wouldn't need the help of Tarzan (whose name by the way, in great ape language, means White Skin), the chief/shaman/medicine man's various antics set up a disturbing question for me and a friend who saw the movie.

As I rolled my eyes and groaned during the bee sequence, my friend, who is also Native, had a substantially different reaction. She shrugged and said: "It's shape-shifting. Our people have it too. I can believe in it." There it was. I was scoffing at this typical Hollywood adventure story, with the clichéd wiseman from deepest, darkest Africa, forgetting that shape-shifting and other such manifestations have long been a part of aboriginal legend and lore.

It put me in a position of trying to figure out, for the first time in a long time, what I actually believe in. Not just about Native (or African, for that matter) shape-shifting, but Christianity and the entire Western belief system. It's just that in our upbringing, in this twentieth century, the stories of shape-shifting and other spiritual beliefs have been relegated to quaint children's stories or stories from a long time past; much like the far-fetched tales of most organized religions have. Then, every once in a while, you meet somebody who really believes. To him or her, it's not a story, it's not a legend. It's reality.

Several years ago I was sitting around a kitchen late one night talking with about six or eight people, most from Manitoulin Island, and most of them women. And through one digression or another, the topic turned to the fabled Little People, the little hairy people of the water. They're a mythical (and I do use the term loosely) people who live in the rocks and cracks around large bodies of fresh water. They travel the water in stone canoes and are very hard to catch a glimpse of.

One after another, each woman would relate stories of the Little People: who in their community had seen one, how they had seen them, why they had seen them. It was an evening of Little People stories. Except that they weren't just stories. Any more than people talking about family relatives or recounting their recent adventures at the bingo hall was just storytelling. The tone, the language, the feeling of the conversation, all told me that these women not only believed in the Little People, but thought of them as a part of everyday life. It was like talking about old friends that came to visit every other year or so.

It's not that I didn't believe in them. It's just that I never took the time to actually think about the Little People, or shape-shifters, or any of the other wonderful and exciting aspects of Native spirituality, on a personal level. I was feeling a bit of a spiritual emptiness. When you don't know what you believe, or how much to believe, it can be a bit of a downer.

I once read an interview with a Native judge who was receiving an award. Recently in the news there had been articles about a Native community banishing a lawbreaker. The punishment for his offenses was time spent alone on an island, in accordance with traditional teachings. The judge was asked how he felt about the resurgence of this form of punishment. This Native judge responded by saying that he respected the decisions of this community but he still preferred the Queen's law. He felt it was a better, more objective system.

To each his own.

Though still plagued by particular questions and a certain amount of skepticism that comes with living in the dominant culture, I've decided to believe rather than disbelieve. Positive is always better than negative. The glass is half full, not half empty. Maybe nobody (more than likely White people) can definitively prove the existence of the Little People or shape-shifters. But the whole point is that nobody has to. I can't prove I have relatives I see every other year. I don't want to. It's nobody's business but my own.

Besides, I want to see if the mighty Tarzan can paddle a stone canoe.

# Checking Under The Bed

For the past six and a half years, it seems I have shared an apartment with some unexpected guests. As luck would have it, the rental Gods had seen fit to bless me with a rather large two story, two bedroom apartment, located on a lovely street in Toronto. What I don't remember seeing in the lease involved some unforeseen boarders living in the second floor room that doubles for the guest bedroom and office. I am a writer and its been in that second floor room where I have created some of my (hopefully) great works of art. Alone, I originally thought.

But unbeknownst to me, somebody or something else had a prior claim to that patch of space—which as a Native person, the irony was not lost upon me. It all started a year or two after I had moved in. A fellow playwright, also Native, was staying in that spare room while in town working on a production. I was away but she later told me about the night she was sitting on the steps, directly underneath the window of the mystery room, having a cigarette. Out of the corner of her eye, she thought she saw a shadow cross the house directly in front of her—meaning the "thing" that cast the shadow came from the room in which she planned to sleep. Puzzled, she watched the house where the shadow had been moments before, only to see it pass by again. Unnerved, she investigated but found nothing. A comfortable night of sleep followed.

Several years later, another friend, this time a Native filmmaker, told me she thought she saw a person in that room once when she too was staying under my roof. It was only a fleeting glance, out of the corner of her eye, but it was enough to make her comment on it to me. She, like the other woman, shrugged it off and nothing else happened.

Now this was where I began to puzzle. While having nothing more than a passing interest in the supernatural, I began wondering

66

if maybe, we had a... dare I say it... ghost in the house. I had never seen what ever this thing was but then again, when I'm in that room, its usually to write, and I become pretty focussed at that time. A walking corpse would have to tap on my shoulder pretty hard to get my attention.

The final, and perhaps most perceptive experience came when my girlfriend's best friend came for a visit. The morning after she spent the night in that room, she calmly asked if we had any "Little People" living in our house. Evidently she had felt "somebody" tugging on her hair as she lay in her bed and assumed that's what they were.

I was not unfamiliar with "Little People." The concept and reputations of "Little People" extends well beyond the famous Irish Leprauchan version. In fact, most cultures around the world have numerous legends detailing the adventures of these diminutive creatures that can live anywhere and everywhere. In this case we are talking of a more Indigenous clan. The multitudes of Native societies existing in Canada and the States are no different in these beliefs. My people, the Ojibway, have many stories about them, so do the Iroquois, my girlfriend and her friend with the tuggable hair.

They are indeed a select bunch. One odd aspect of these miniature inhabitants is that, to my knowledge, they have only revealed themselves to Native women, at least in my house. All three of my guests were Native women. Maybe they have a predilection for the double X chromosomes. Or perhaps the men who have stayed in that room don't have hair long enough to tug. Two of the three were artists of one sort or another, the other a student. Maybe they were more open to the possibility. Accountants or stockbrokers might not be so receptive. But regardless, as a sign of respect, I have been very careful with mousetraps.

But this issue is fast becoming an irrelevant point. For in the next few weeks, we will be moving. A new house beckons, on a new street, with new adventures. But I must not be too confident. Little People can move too. Maybe they will decide to join us in our new house. Or maybe they will stay behind and play games on the next tenants. The will of these tiny dwellers are unfathomable to us people of a more blessed vertical stature.

As is the custom of my people, we will put down a little

tobacco when we leave, as a parting gift to them. We hope they will accept it and remember us fondly. Or they might consider it a bribe to travel with us. What ever their decision is, we will accept it.

But one thing does bother me, Little People or ghosts... they were there in the room with me as I wrote and struggled with many different writing projects. Often I would reach a dead end, or face writer's block as I stared at a blank computer screen. Then suddenly, out of nowhere, I would receive a flash of inspiration. It wouldn't be long before I found myself typing "The End." So if my unforeseen houseguests were responsible for such stimuli, does that make them my ghost writers?

# The Bomb Waiting

Tick, tick, tick. The older I get, the louder that relentless reminder becomes. Each year, each day: tick, tick. Evidence of this internal biological bomb is everywhere around me: my family, the news, government statistics. Inside of me, a Native man in his mid-thirties, lies a ticking bomb. Dormant for the moment, thank God, I know it lies there waiting for the biochemical fuse to be lit.

What was once unknown to most Native people, has almost become inevitable. Diabetes is a full-blown epidemic in most Native families and communities. A recent study taken in the small northern Ontario Aboriginal community of Sandy Lake showed that almost twenty-nine percent of the population was diabetic, with another fourteen percent showing the early symptoms. That's forty-three percent. And that's just one village. Tick, tick.

While working on a project in Pennsylvania last summer, I saw a documentary on the Pima people located somewhere down in the American Southwest. For uncountable centuries these people eked a living in the desert, drawing water from a small river nearby. As with many of their neighbours, their diet was high in grain and vegetables, with a little meat thrown in. Refined or store-bought food was a rarity.

Then sometime during the 1930s, the American government felt the need to divert the river, the lifeblood of the community, in another direction. Robbed of their water, the Pima were also robbed of their ability to provide their own food. Feeling responsible, the government stepped in and began providing the community with relief supplies and provisions. Needless to say, much of it consisted of canned meat, processed food, and sugar.

Sixty years later, the diabetes rate is almost fifty percent, with one quarter suffering from some physical ailment brought on by the disease, and one in ten having had some form of amputation due to the condition. Obesity is the norm.

These are just statistics, and statistics are meaningless. Faceless numbers that are delightfully removed from most people's everyday existence. I know. I've ignored a lot of statistics. Then I began to hear that sound coming from my body.

Tick, tick, tick.

Last Christmas I was at my Aunt's house on my Reserve. I was there with several members of my family enjoying dessert after a hearty Christmas meal. Various pies and cakes were being passed around when one of my uncles mentioned how this was going to affect his blood-sugar level. As I sat there, with a huge slab of apple pie on my lap, I saw the conversation take a decidedly different turn. This was a room full of my aunts and uncles, all of whom were casually comparing and discussing the various levels of insulin they all take. I felt the pie on my lap getting heavier.

Of the thirteen surviving children my grandparents had, six, including my mother, are diabetic. That's a little over forty-six percent. Higher than in Sandy Lake. Tick, tick.

I didn't even know my mother suffered from the disease until I visited her in the hospital for a minor operation several years ago. As she lay there in her bed, I noticed the identification tag on her wrist. It indicated the patient was a diabetic. Concerned for my mother's welfare, I was going to report the potentially dangerous mislabeling to a nurse, but my mother assured me it was no mistake. She was a diabetic. So was my grandmother. The affliction had found them both late in their lives and these things were always viewed as a private matter.

That's why the Christmas incident caught me by surprise. It was the first such conversation of that sort I can remember hearing. People are talking and acting—facing it. There are now full-time Aboriginal diabetes health workers and workshops. Before, in my youth, I'd never heard of such things, let alone a need for them.

I still hear the ticking, and it does worry me, but I manage to hold that omnipresent sound at a distance. There's a good chance, somewhere over fifty percent, that it will pass me by.

Those are dangerous odds.

Luckily I don't have much of a sweet-tooth, unlike one relative I grew up watching put four tablespoons of sugar into her coffee. My only weakness consists largely of soft drinks and the occasional bowl of ice cream. Still...

There's an old saying about death and taxes being the only things you can really count on in this world. Well, most Native people who live on Reserves don't pay a lot of taxes. Maybe for them, and for me, it's death and diabetes that are the reality these days.

Tick, tick, tick.

# A Modest, Tongue-in-Cheek Proposal

A friend of mine was recently telling me about a conference he attended some time back. At this same conference, where there were Native people from across all the Americas, he found himself talking with a Kayapo Indian from Brazil. In the spirit of striking up an innocent conversation with this fellow Aboriginal, he good-naturedly asked the Kayapo gentleman what his impression was of Canada's Native people. Without missing a beat, the first thing the man said he noticed was "they're all so fat!" I'm told those were his exact words.

The point to this awkward, though true, little story... on the same day I was told of this brief exchange, I had just gotten back from my first Powwow of the season. There, in one single day, I had consumed enough calories and fat, albeit all too willingly, in my diet (and I use the term loosely), to kill a dozen vegetarians (with a few "I-only-eat-chicken-or-fish" types thrown in). Late that night, while I lay there digesting, I was kept awake by the sounds of my arteries hardening. A sound similar to ice cracking on a frozen lake. Or a nice juicy hamburger crackling on a hot grill!

And while I kept a constant vigil on my pulse throughout the night, I had a vision. Actually it might have been a nightmare brought on by too much hot sauce on one of the Indian tacos I had sampled that day. But the vision was there regardless. I don't quite know if the Native population is ready for it, but I think it merits some discussion. With all the high levels of diabetes and obesity evident in many of our Native communities, I offer to the Aboriginal community... the concept of the Low-fat Powwow!

I know the notion of a Low-fat Powwow makes about as much sense as a non-smoking bingo, but it may not be as far-fetched as it sounds. Just examine the idea a bit closer. It's all there, possible, and waiting.

For the head dancer, I propose the fast-dancing, always-on-the-move weight-loss guru Richard Simmons. He's from the States, he must have some Cherokee or Choctaw blood in him. Hell, everybody I've ever met from the States claims to have some. And for the Female Elder, how about Jenny Craig, proprietor of all those weight-loss clinics? Between those two, every deep fryer in the land would be sweating grease, for sure.

Of course, some of the dancing styles might have to be modified slightly. I kind of like the concept of creating special classes of dancing for the health conscious—how does the aerobic "Fancy" sound to you? "Shake that regalia. And three more, and two more, and one more, and twirl."

And then there's the low-impact "Jingle." "Three jingles to the left, three jingles to the right, and stop." How about some high-cardio grass dancing to eat up those annoying calories?

But exercise would only be the first step. There are other hurdles (no calisthenics pun intended) to overcome. Somehow I can't see Powwow patrons beating a path to a food stand that carries delicacies like tofu on a scone, or lemonade with no sugar. Boy, that would pucker you right up. Even Sweet n' Low lemonade doesn't sound quite right.

How about corn soup with a good, healthy seaweed stock instead of salt pork? Instead of gravy on your fries, how about alfalfa sprouts? And of course I have yet to see a veggie-burger at any Powwow stand. The Native philosophy behind that? "Put the vegetables inside the cow first, then we'll eat them." I think I saw that on a Powwow t-shirt once.

And after the Powwow, instead of going to sing 49er songs all night, smoking and partying to the late hours of the morning, might I suggest a little Powwow karaoke? Have all the music pre-taped and somebody can just walk in and order up a song and let loose with a good crow-hop tune. Or maybe somebody has a hankering to sing an inter-tribal. The guy in the fringe jacket sure can belt out a Sneak Up song. Good clean, healthy fun.

But then again, although this all might be healthier, it wouldn't be a Powwow, now would it? I probably wouldn't go to it. No, I think I'll just do an extra half-hour on the stairmaster, or, in my case, the Native equivalent, running up and down the front steps. Or maybe I'll do an hour. That way I can get some fries with extra grease. And as I eat them lovingly one by one, I will be thinking to myself: "and three more, and two more and one..."

# Are You a Chip Off the Old Block?

Emerging from the bowels of Curve Lake (a cool, hip Indigenous place), a new name in fashion has been born, nursed on cotton, and weaned on thread. Called CHIP, (short for Cool Hip Indigenous Person), this line of shirts, hats, shorts, and various sports attire has already been taking the Powwow and tournament scene by storm.

But unbeknownst to the owners/designers, Brad Castel and Tanya Leary, a unique problem concerning the concept of fashion and culture has arisen from this company's stitching. It seems before one can wear a CHIP shirt or shorts, it has become mandatory to first be classified as, and be able to prove that you are, a member of the Cool Hip Indigenous People.

From an undisclosed inside source, I have learned that upon the purchase of an article of clothing, you are asked to fill out a questionnaire. Based on the information contained in that completed questionnaire, it will be decided if you command the necessary attributes to be considered one of the Cool Hip Indigenous People, and if indeed you are worthy enough to be the proud owner of a CHIP product.

That same clandestine and undercover source, whom I call Deep Pockets, has seen fit to secretly supply me with a sample of the actual questionnaire. The following survey questions are the new standards by which a Cool Hip Indigenous Person is being judged today. Are you one of them?

You are not a Cool Hip Indigenous Person if you:

• wear plaid or flannel of any kind
• you do not care that when it comes to weight and bellies, size does matter
• suffer from bingo-dabber calluses

75

- if you consider the cartoon movie *Pocahontas* a serious depiction of Aboriginal life
- consider Kraft Dinner a "traditional" Aboriginal meal
- own more than one "Indian Motorcycle" shirt or sweater
- have memorized one or any of the verses from the song "Kaliga"
- if you think Oka is just a type of cheese
- voted for the Reform Party
- believe that when in doubt, "fry it"

You are a Cool Hip Indigenous Person if you:

- can properly pronounce all the Kashtin's songs correctly
- can remember Captain Kirk's character's name when he thought he was an Indian in an episode of *Star Trek*
- you can tell the difference in taste between a woodland caribou and a tundra-fed caribou
- know which Great Lake Manitoulin Island is located in
- can name all six of the Six Nations, and know which is the most recent
- can handle a canoe regardless of its construction material (birchbark, fibreglass, wood, porcelain, video game)
- can say "hello" or any form of greeting in at least four Indigenous languages
- can say "cool, hip, Indigenous, person" in any Indigenous language
- are aware that true Native art is not manufactured all the way in the Far East (Micmacs excluded)
- if your Indigenous hips are personally pretty cool

Of course there are all sorts of possible combinations and characteristics based on your response to the survey. For instance, you can be partially cool, slightly hip, maybe kind of Indigenous, and fractionally a person. Feel free to mix and match your favourite Aboriginal attributes.

In fact, you could be an Indigenous half-breed, or a hip Métis (of sorts), a full-blooded person, or maybe your great-grandmother was partially cool.

76

# No Time For Indian Time

If there's one thing I (and I'm sure a g'jillion others) hate in this world, it's stereotypes. No surprise there. In fact, much of the work I do as a playwright and journalist deals with addressing those inaccurate and often damaging images, particularly the Native ones. But if there's even one more thing in this world I hate more then afore-mentioned stereotypes, it's people who use those stereotypes, quite often of themselves, as an excuse for their poor behaviour.

I was recently in Vancouver where a play of mine, with several Native actors in the cast, was in production. During the rehearsal, one of actors was proving annoyingly difficult for not having the ability to show up on time for rehearsals and run-throughs. A decidedly naughty no-no in the world of theatre, not to mention any other respectable business. Needless to say several stern lectures were administered to the actor. Several days later, his best friend, oddly enough a non-Native person, phoned the theatre office to complain. He accused the company of being racist and not understanding that Native people are "culturally unable to be on time." Evidently, he informed the office staff, the Aboriginal people of this country are ethnically and racially late for everything and the company was being unsympathetic in its inability to recognize and respect that cultural quirk. Basically, forcing Native people to watch the clock was a form of colonial oppression.

One of the people who took the call was a Native woman. One, whom I believe, was never late for work. This simple fact, strongly delivered by this stranger on the phone, seemed to surprise her, as it did me. I was not aware that being tardy was one of those Aboriginal rights constantly being argued about in treaties.

This concept, commonly known as "Indian time," is quite popular and well-exercised in the Native community. And on most occasions, it serves a logical purpose. The concept behind "Indian

Time" is that things start or happen when they need to, not by some artificial beginning. There is no need to rush something that does not have to be rushed. A Powwow Grand Entry is supposed to start at 12:00, if it starts at 1:00, it is not worth having a heart attack. If people are an hour or two late for a party or some other gathering, nobody panics. Time is not rigid. That is true "Indian Time" and I practice that myself.

But often, some people use this ancient concept to escape or shift blame for the carelessness of their actions. If there is a meeting or some important event that has repercussions beyond this individual, and they are late, I've heard them shrug it off blaming it on "Indian Time" and not taking responsibility for it themselves. I wonder if any of these people have ever tried to catch a train or plane. I also wonder if they would be as nonchalant if their paycheque was a little late due to "head-office time."

What makes this so annoying is that traditionally Native people did respect time. If a trip was planned for dawn, it was guaranteed people would be ready to depart in the canoes when the sun first peaked over the horizon. Those that practiced "Indian Time" had better have an extra pair of moccasins for the long walk ahead of them.

Same with the first sighting of a buffalo herd or the arrival of migratory ducks and geese. Its not in the nature of these animals to hang around waiting for people to find the time to kill them. The Native people had to be able to move and react instantly. Nature waits for no people.

That's why I've always had a problem with those who abuse the concept of "Indian Time." My mother, who has spent most of her life on the Reserve, her first language is Ojibway, and can be classified as being as "Indian" as anybody, prides herself on never being late for an appointment. Most of the time she's early. There's nothing more annoying for a young Native boy than your mother making sure you're early for a dentist appointment. But since this West Coast gentleman and his friend seem to believe that being late is "culturally correct," my mother must not be that Native. That will be a surprise to her.

Lillian McGregor, a well respected Elder currently living in Toronto, perhaps put it best when she talked about a watch she bought with her first paycheque. "This watch is very meaningful for me as it taught me to value time, both mine and that of others. I learned that promptness was a form of respect. I grasped how quickly time passed and that each hour, minute and second was a gift from the Creator."

Maybe somebody should buy this young actor from the West a watch.

# White May Not Be Right

You mention that somebody is in a black mood, or perhaps a friend of yours has a red-hot temper, and you can immediately get a grasp of the temperament of the individual you are talking about. Colour, for the longest time, has often been used as a descriptive element in describing the emotional and moral fibre of people, places and things. But, oddly enough, it seems the darker the colour mentioned, the more dangerous or ominous those people, places and things become.

For instance, if you notice bad, stormy weather by remarking how dark the skies look, or if you've heard the Devil referred to as the "Lord of Darkness," you'll get my point. I looked up the word "black" in a dictionary that partially defined the word as gloomy or dismal, sullen or hostile, evil or wicked, and indicative of disgrace.

Yet, you mention the word "white," and a completely different concept emerges: images of purity, virginity, cleanliness immediately pop to mind. In fact, just recently in a newspaper I came across the phrase "linen-white landscape," used to describe an earlier, more innocent era of time. Let us not forget the famous "little white lie" which means doing something wrong for the right (or white) reasons. Ancient racial intolerance and biases are more than likely at work here.

But what I find so ironic is that when you actually look at the pigment of the many things available to modern Canadians today, the opposite is true. Especially when it comes to the tasty world of food. Many of the most dangerous, most unhealthy, and most evil edibles we consume are in fact white in colour. Your cupboards are potential death traps. There may be a need for rigorous readjustment of colour perceptions in the near future.

The colour white may do its most widespread damage in the world of edibles and nourishment. Practically everything white used in the culinary arts has been confirmed as being dangerous to one's health. Sugar has long been viewed as a menace. Salt is like playing with a loaded gun. White rice, while not particularly dangerous, is basically viewed as a pot of unhelpful starch. Each dab of cream or whole milk can be viewed as a potential nail in your coffin.

Need I mention the reputation white flour has in the health community? Add to that its many by-products—white bread and the like—and we're talking empty calories with little nutritional benefits. Might as well inject the glucose directly into your thighs and waist. Why waste (no pun intended) time on the stomach?

And finally, at the top of the pallid pyramid lie fat and the infamous brick of lard (basically rendered fat). Both are white, and both are notoriously bad for your health. Unless heart disease and strokes appeal to you. Death does indeed ride a pale horse.

What I find equally scary is the realization that one of the most common and trusted forms of sustenance known to Native people—the proud, mighty, and eternal bannock/frybread/scone—is, in fact, made of white flour, white sugar, white salt, and white baking powder, and is usually fried in white lard. I am a great believer in tradition, but I do not think it would be disrespectful to consider, perhaps, throwing a vitamin or two into the mix.

And taking a slight detour, but still on the subject of "not really good for you," I do believe heroin is white in colour, although I am no expert on the subject, I assure you. Cocaine and crack are also that familiar milky hue, if I'm not mistaken. And let us not forget the ever-popular white rum. If the more innocent past can be "linen-white," I assume the more jaded present may be alluded to as having a "heroin-white landscape."

And yet, on the other hand, the darker the shade of these same foodstuffs, the more beneficial they are perceived to be for your body. Brown sugar, or even honey, is observed to be better than its white counterpart. The same goes with brown rice, and whole wheat flour and bread. I'm not sure where the jury stands on dark rum though.

Casting our net a little wider, there are numerous other ivory-toned purveyors of pain and death out there in the world. It would take far too long to mention all of them... but how about the Great White shark and the polar bear, both having a reputation for the most

81

attacks on humans? Then there's Melville's "Moby Dick," the great white whale, the KKK… the list goes on and on.

At the risk of sounding racist (which I'm not—I'm more of a foodist), it looks pretty much like everything white is bad for you. It makes you wonder what all those White supremacists are so damn proud of.

# Who's to Blame and Who Has the Right to Blame?

I have a great respect for those who have educated themselves and have taken the time to think about the world and their place in it as both individuals and as Native people in general. But every once in a while you bump into people who have taken that education, and those wonderfully complex thoughts, and have done strange and questionable things with them.

Case in point: While attending an Aboriginal academic conference, I happened to be part of an informal gathering where a friend of mine, in conversation with several other scholarly Aboriginals, expressed her confusion over White people's—or those we call the Colour Challenged—die-hard refusal to accept guilt or culpability for what has happened in the five hundred and six years of colonialism. Basically, but severely paraphrased, she said "When are White people going to accept their guilt for what their ancestors have done? I don't think they seriously understand their responsibility." Somewhere deep inside me, I could feel DNA picking sides.

These words, and the meanings behind them, reverberated within my head. I don't know if it was simply my White half that rebelled against such a broad statement (when asked, I tell people every other cell in my body is Caucasian), or if my own inherent Aboriginal sensibility questioned the accuracy of that belief. While I was raised Native, in a Native community, with no connection to my non-Native half, I am still conscious of it. My friend is a very smart person, with clear-cut beliefs, but also a gentle and well-liked individual. I respect her greatly. But that understood, I wondered where I stood in the wide spectrum of accusations inherent in her statements.

My problem, I think, is that I have trouble assigning complete blame to an entire race. To me, it harks back to the Germans and the Jews. It's a brutal comparison, I grant you, but fifty years ago the

Nazi party attributed blame for the ills of the Depression and a multitude of other social problems in Germany specifically to the Jews. Today, equally unfairly, many have painted Germans rather broadly for the actions of some of their ancestors.

So, to say all White people are to blame makes me incredibly uncomfortable. Where would my friend and her associates begin to lay blame? With all ashen-complexioned people in general? What about White people who themselves were discriminated against? Like, for instance, the Irish and Scottish, who have a long history of repression, or again, the Jews (though I've heard some argue about whether Jews can be classified as Caucasian). What about immigrants in general? I recently met a Bosnian woman who had just moved to Canada. I do believe I noticed her skin being of the milky shade. Is she to be included in the blame?

Or is there a residency requirement before blame is extended, much like health benefits? Ten years maybe? twenty? How about thirty? Or perhaps we should be counting generations instead. Must the pallid-enhanced person be first generation Canadian? Second? Definitely third or fourth I'm sure. I'm a little fuzzy as to where the line of guilt begins. I won't even go into all the White people I've met who claim they were Native in another life. Actually, if pressed, I would say, "well, you're not one now."

On a realistic level, when I go to my local Second Cup for my daily latte and am served by a gangly, pimple-faced teenager, I just can't seem to look at him and think "You, as a member of the pigment-challenged majority, are personally responsible for my Reserve having only a few thousand square acres to call home, when once we roamed freely across the land." The fact that he probably works for minimum wage makes it even more difficult.

Another provocative statement to be issued by my friend is even more politically volatile in nature: "It's impossible for Native people, or people of any other minority, to be racist. Only White people can be racist. You can only be racist looking down, not up." Again, I'm sure there's some legitimate pseudo-political understanding behind that declaration. I'm just not sure I want to know what it is.

Because of the academic psychobabble that interspersed the conversation, it seemed to me that a fancy, academic coating was covering old-fashioned intolerance. Paraphrasing a fable, the Emperor may have new clothes. But he's still naked. Disliking someone because of the colour of their skin or their cultural background works both ways. At least that's what I've always been taught by my Elders. I realize I might be incredibly naive about all of this, but I just don't see how it's okay, even acceptable, to discriminate one way, but not another. Maybe you learn these things in university.

I am aware that I am probably boiling these complicated and intricate sociopolitical arguments down to overly simplistic terms. Tough. I like simple terms. How many of us operate our lives in strictly sociopolitical environments? How many of us would want to? I certainly don't. I like to think I live in the real world with real people. I learned long ago that the more blame you assign to other people, the more blame you accumulate yourself. It's an Aboriginal karma thing.

However, I don't want people to think I am letting the dominant culture off the hook for past injustices. Not by a long shot. The Status Card I carry with me all the time is a constant reminder that there are still a multitude of concerns to be dealt with by the government and society at large. All I'm saying is beware of the shoe that fits on the other foot. And maybe the moccasin too.

I heard it best put at a discussion I attended in Montreal several years ago. One person-of-pallor stood defiantly and asked a row of Native people seated at the front table how long they expected him to feel guilty for what his ancestors had done.

The table spokesman said quietly, "No, I don't expect you to feel guilty for what your ancestors have done. However, if things haven't changed in twenty years, then I expect you to feel guilty."

I hope they teach that in university.

# It Loses Something in the Translation

With the onslaught of political correctness in recent years, the term "Indian" has rapidly gone out of favour in referring to Canada's original inhabitants. Instead, a plethora of "colourful" terms, such as Native, Aboriginal, First Nations, and even Indigenous, are currently used as both adjectives and nouns in the ongoing battle to properly describe us. Even when we talk about ourselves, there is some dissension.

But the English language, now used by the vast majority of Native people, and the words we have chosen for self description in these more enlightened times, are no better than "Indian," that ubiquitous "sub-continent" term from by-gone days. In fact, many find the numerous Aboriginal-related terms' correctness suspect and their usage questionable. Unfortunately, it can be confusing being an English-speaking First Nations person.

The term First Nations, to me, is a political phrase, often used to describe what used to be called a Reserve. For instance, I come from the Curve Lake First Nation. But personally, I am a little uncomfortable being called a First Nations person because I do not consider myself a political term. Therefore to say I am First Nations limits me to a strictly political nature or definition. And who wants that? Cynics will argue that everything is political. Especially being Native in Canada. But I would still rather be a person than a political definition. Call me a rebel if you will.

The other term of questionable description is the familiar expression "Aboriginal." Deconstructing the word, the prefix "ab," used in such other well-known words as abominable (as in the abominable snowman), abhorrent, absurd, abysmal, abnormal, abscess, abase, abject, to name a few, all have a negative connotation. They all seem to denote a certain pessimistic designation or flavour to what ever is being discussing. Thus, being an Aboriginal is not a very flattering term. But it does beg the question "Could the Inuit of the Arctic be called the Aboriginal snowmen?"

Taking this issue a bit further, I was once sitting in the office of the Native Student Coordinator for a large university. I accidentally overheard the coordinator talking on the phone with a new student that was interested in coming in for a chat. I heard a familiar phrase being issued by this keeper of the office: "Are you of Native descent?" The immediate image in my mind was of a Native person taking an escalator to the basement. Descent makes me think of descending. Therefore, being of Native descent is a step downwards. I think we should take command of this language that has taken command of us; I prefer to think of myself as being of Native ascent. I think others should too. I, as well as our people, want to go up in the world, not down.

Above and beyond personal definitions of our culture, the intermingling of Native and non-Native realities, as often occurs through English usage, never fails to amaze me. Several times a year I get invited to various Native Awareness Weeks across the country, usually at universities (no doubt with descending Native students). The irony of the term "awareness" occurred to me one day as I was driving through a small town on my way to such an event. A large banner across the main street alerted the residents that this was also Cancer Awareness Week. In another town I visited recently it was Aids Awareness Week. Still others advertised Diabetes Awareness Week.

And here I was going to Native Awareness Week. Perhaps, with enough money and research, there will be no more need for these Awareness Weeks and these evil scourges will officially be wiped out for ever. My donation is in the mail.

There also seems to be a noticeable gulf in the interpretations of certain words in both cultures. The most obvious to me occurred during the editing of a new book I had coming out. The publisher wrote some promo material and asked me to proof it. I read it over several times but found myself concerned with a certain passage— one word, in fact—that I felt was misleading and could possibly be construed as inappropriate.

I argued with the publisher for several minutes before the misunderstanding became quite evident. The line itself read "...big questions of heritage, family, cultural context and personal identity are ruthlessly stripped of their traditional meanings and become so much useless, embarrassing roadkill on the highway of life."

It was the word "traditional" that I felt was both misleading and inappropriate. I was reading the word from a specifically Native perspective, and taking that into account, the quote sounds somewhat harsh and provocative. Judge for yourself. But the publisher was using the term "traditional" in the context of what is generally believed or accepted. Once we both realized this, we merely changed "traditional" to "conventional," and both went away happy little literary people.

English has been with Native people for just a few centuries now. And it's no secret there has always been a communication problem in one form or another. On the cusp of the millennium, the battle still continues.

# STRANGE BEDFELLOWS
## (POLITICS, SCHMOLITICS [AN ANCIENT OJIBWAY WORD])

# The 1997 Federal Election

On a warm and inviting morning—June 2, 1997, to be exact—I lost my political virginity at the tender age of thirty-four. To an older woman. An "attached" woman at that. I am, of course, talking about that ravishing creature known as Alexa McDonough.

Up until that fateful morning—just yesterday—I must confess to the world that I, Drew Hayden Taylor, have never voted in my life. Not in a federal, provincial, or municipal election, not even in a Band election on my Reserve. My ballot had been uncast, waiting for the right candidate.

Now I think it's important to say that I'm not the most political of people. I can barely spell Alexa McDonough. Is it Mc or Mac? Or is she Micmac? Just kidding. So why did I choose that NDP hell-cat from the East Coast while the rest of the country has chosen the sweet wooing of that "little guy from Shawinigan"? I don't know. Who can say what motivates the passions of voters? Not I.

The ironic thing is that I don't even consider myself particularly "left wing." Don't get me wrong, I'm not particularly "right" either. It's just that in the broad political spectrum of Canadian politics, I consider myself outside the normal parameters. Being Native, I like to think of myself as being a "red wing."

So why did I vote for Alexa and her loyal followers when there is, I believe, at least one Native Member of Parliament who has sworn allegiance to Jean Chretien and the Liberal Party? I mean, how can you not admire the resourcefulness of a guy who used an Inuit sculpture to defend himself against a deranged intruder? Jean: Warrior Prime Minister. It's just a pity that's become the only practical use for art amongst politicians. But I'm not bitter.

And what about Preston Manning and the Reform Party? Well, according to many Native beliefs, the West is believed to be the "Land of the Dead." I won't even go into that.

91

Charest and Duceppe? Duceppe wasn't running in Ontario, he was actually running from Ontario. And some, more cruel than I, would say Charest and his party weren't running on this planet.

All this means is that after all these years of living a politically celibate life, I can no longer wear white. And again, we're back to the question of why Alexa? Is it just because she's the lesser of evils? No, that would be too cynical. After much soul-searching and introspection, I came up with the only logical reason I could find. My girlfriend told me to. Hey, it's as good a reason as any.

# Richman, Poorman—The Only Ones Having Fun

It seems that practically everyday, some member of the financial community or a social service individual is lamenting the growing gulf between the "have's" and "have-not's". Basically, it seems there are more poor people around these days, and, at the same time, more rich, and the middle class blokes are the ones that are suffering because of this.

And it's not just the people in positions of knowledge who are debating these issues. People on the streets are developing their own theories. Just the other day a piece of street philosophy struck me broadside of the ear. I was on my way home when I couldn't help overhearing, on the far sidewalk, a conversation in process. A woman, dressed almost entirely in black leather and arguing quite fervently with what appeared to be her boyfriend, said quite loudly "It's true. Only the rich and the poor can afford to have sex." She didn't actually say "sex," she used a more vernacular term that rhymes with a certain waterfowl, but you get the basic picture.

And as they disappeared down the street, I was haunted by her statement. Haunted by the way, weirdly enough, it made sense. After some meditation, I found myself believing it.

The poor, when not fighting to survive, have no particular job to spend their days at, no pastimes that occupy the hours of the day. So, what else are you going to do when you don't have to waste your time worrying about that second mortgage? And unlike movies, golf, and other popular pastimes, sex doesn't usually involve an admission fee or membership dues. At least not where I come from. You could say it's an economically unbiased activity. Hell, you can even do it by yourself if you don't have a partner.

The rich, on the other hand, have a multitude of people to do everything for them: the laundry, the kids' carpool, the cooking, the cleaning, the pool maintenance, tax evasion. With such a support staff, that leaves plenty of free time, no doubt in satin or silk sheets, available for the art of sex. But from what I understand, it is rarely with poor people. Which is a pity since it could potentially create a bond that would unite the two disparate fiscal groups. It would beat the hell out of an economic conference.

Obviously, this leaves out the lamentable, over-occupied, and frustrated middle-class that, evidently, has too little available time on its hands to put anything interesting into its hands. Between working overtime to buy the second car (probably that adorable new VW Beetle), attending PTA meetings (a by-product of when this populace was younger, poorer, and had the time for sex), and collecting canned goods for the poor (who are too busy having sex to collect it themselves), the nights fall with an exhausted thump. These people end up falling asleep in front of their satellite television with a Heineken in their hand.

Keeping all of this in mind, it quickly becomes rather obvious why the ranks of the rich and poor are swelling (no pun intended). What do you expect when the rich and the poor are the only ones "doing it"! There's a reason the middle-class is disappearing. And it has nothing to do with taxes, because I'm not sure of a way the government could possibly tax this. Frequency? Duration? Satisfaction? Location?

But perhaps the middle-class should contemplate an evening with one less dinner party, one less night at the theatre or weekend at the cottage, and stick to the basics of home entertainment. That might help lessen the gulf between the fortunate and unfortunate. I'm all for doing my bit for the cause.

From the Aboriginal perspective, this theory adds a certain amount of logic towards explaining why the vast majority of Native people in this country live in crushing poverty. Yet we have one of the highest, if not the highest, birth rate in the country. And fifty percent of the over one million Native people are under twenty-five. I guess you could say it pays to be poor.

It beats the hell out of a Volkswagen bug.

# Commentary

Jobs, national unity, the deficit: all important issues of the upcoming federal election, to be sure. But am I the only one that can't help noticing that there seems to be a very important issue absent from the various political platforms? One that, shall we say, reeks of sweet-grass and bingo halls.

Granted, it may be the fact that I grew up on a Native Reserve, have an Ojibway mother, and have spent a lifetime wondering how to place a land claim on the Parliament buildings that has made it obvious to me that yet again, the Native people, and the multitude of issues surrounding their lives and very existence, are, as usual, being completely ignored by the candidates.

I understand that in the grand political scheme, I may simply be a one-issue potential voter but sometimes one issue is all it takes to sway elections. Considering there are almost two million Canadians out there in electorate land that claim some sort of Aboriginal heritage, me thinks the candidates should prick up their ears before they get a political arrow in the back. After all, we are too sizable a population to ignore.

Watching the campaign trail as I have, it seems that the politicians can conveniently overlook the pressing Native issues of the day at will, until it gets to the point where somebody picks up a gun and waves it about. Then it becomes a law-and-order issue and they wash their hands of the whole thing. Witness Gustafsen Lake and Ipperwash. A little political expediency early on in those matters might have saved lives and costly trials.

Take the Royal Commission on Aboriginal Peoples for example. The title sounds impressive but where is it today, over six months after it was released? When it came out, I and a lot of Native and non-Native people had high hopes for this long-anticipated document. But those dreams soon sank like Bre-X stock. A fifty million-dollar placebo for the Native population of Canada. Its final destination as reading material is probably in the bathrooms of Chretien, Charest, and the rest. The only way they'll find the time to read the whole thing is if they get their hands on some bad pâté.

As a Native person I'm not asking for a lot. I just want it to be shown that I matter in this election. That these politicians are talking to me. If this keeps up, we just have to start our own political party, and then they'll have to listen to us as we give evasive answers on all their issues. Imagine an entire election with no mention of national unity or the deficit. And we'd have a real "red book" to offer.

# Half Empty or Half Full

Not long ago I received a letter from a woman whom I shall call Lynda. Unfortunately the envelope with her return address has been lost in transit. In this letter she struggled to share some of the anger and confusion she felt at being a person trapped between two cultures. She was a product of an Irish mother and a Mohawk father; they had evidently separated when she was young and, as a result, she had practically no contact with her Aboriginal roots during her adolescence.

She writes: "I still feel I have to somehow prove a connectedness with full-Natives in order for me to be accepted... I feel like I'm in a nowhere zone of cultural identity... I've had some very ignorant remarks made towards me by non-Natives, but what really hurts is being shunned by full-Natives and Native organizations." One Elder even questioned the existence of her Reserve, the Mohawk community of Tyendinaga in southern Ontario. "Never heard of it" she said to Lynda and turned away.

Anybody who is familiar with my work knows that I pride myself on being an "Occasian," somebody of Ojibway and Caucasian ancestry. I have written quite extensively on that particular subject, both examining the issue from a personal point of view and sometimes joking about the concept. As an Elder once told me, "You either are something or you aren't. You can't be half. But it is possible to be two things, not just one."

Lynda, wherever you may be, I went through the same thing you did. I have bluish eyes and a fair complexion, but one of the few characteristics I do seem to share with my Native family is my troublesome belly that keeps showing that Native fondness for high-calorie food.

Most of my life I grew up with: "you're not Native, are you?" and "You don't look it," and a dozen other variations. Recently I was walking down the street and a Native panhandler accosted me for money. Being in a hurry for a meeting, I waved him off. As I hustled away, he saw the First Nations jacket I was wearing and screamed after me "First Nations! I don't think so!" Another time I was entering a money machine alcove in a bank. There was a young Native woman standing there warming herself. She took one look at my jacket, sneered and said: "What tribe, Wannabe?"

My advice to Lynda? Get used to it. I don't mean that to sound harsh but for every one of those types of people out there, I have met a thousand who will welcome you. It just seems that sometimes in the great balance of life, the ratio of good to bad will get a little erratic and bunch up on the bad side. Sometimes it will seem like the "unbelievers" are the only kind of people you'll meet.

One final note of confidence. What these people are failing to acknowledge is that it's pretty well accepted that after five hundred and five years of occupation and intermarriage, there are precious few individuals out there who can claim complete full-blooded Native ancestry. They're just seeing in you what they refuse to see in themselves.

Lynda, I know of Tyendinaga. I hear all the best people come from there.

# Megacity

Recently I was approached by a member of an organization Citizens for Local Democracy and asked to join them in their crusade against the Tories' pet project, the Megacity. If successful, this will, in effect, combine the existing cities of Toronto, Scarborough, Etobicoke, North York, York, and the borough of East York to form one large super-city.

Now, I'm the Artistic Director of a Native theatre company—Native Earth Performing Arts, to be exact—and I guess it's always a good idea to have the support of a high profile multicultural organization behind you. And to be honest, the humour and irony of the situation was not lost upon us: an association consisting mostly of White people, coming to a Native organization to seek assistance in preventing their land from being taken away. As we Native people say, life is truly a circle. And as for the Megacity itself, it could be just me, but doesn't the name sound like the newest Canadian superhero? Megacity: friend to those who have no friends; enemy to those who have no enemies. Just when you thought it was safe to move back to Toronto… MEGACITY!

Anyway, from the Native perspective, Mike Harris's one-big-city concept does have a certain amount of, dare I say, logic to it if you examine the origins of the word "Toronto." To the uninformed, Toronto is an Iroquois word meaning "the gathering or meeting place." I wonder if Mr. Harris had that in mind when he came up with his amalgamation idea. Did he bring all the mayors together in his office and say "Hey gang, let's all gather and meet here as one big happy family?" Somehow I doubt it.

But there is an even bigger ironic twist to all of this controversy. I know something most of the Tories, and probably the rest of the Greater Toronto area inhabitants, have forgotten. Amalgamation may be a forgone conclusion. Regardless of what the Premier has up his sleeve, chances are that Toronto and many of the other local cities will be all lumped together sometime in the future anyway—if the people of the Mississauga Nation have their way. For those with short memories, that's the Native band that has a very large land claim on much of Toronto and its adjacent areas. Think of it as sort of an Aboriginal amalgamation. Metaphorically, it's better for the Mississauga Nation to get the whole pie, rather than all the slices individually. So thanks Mike, for doing all the paper work.

# The Dating Game—Who Should Date Whom in the Native Community

The last time I was in Edmonton I got asked the question again. It's a question I find myself getting asked quite frequently, as if I am the spokesperson for all Native men in Canada (if I am, I want a better salary). And to tell you the truth, it's getting annoying. This time it happened on a radio talk show hosted by a Native woman. Logically, it is always a Native woman who asks this question.

"Why is it that Native men, when they reach a certain level of success and power, end up dating and marrying only White women, and not Native women?"

Often they point to Ovide Mercredi, Graham Greene, Tom Jackson, etc., as examples. All well known, prosperous men whose partners are of the Caucasian persuasion. This is a question and issue that is of specific interest to many Native women, who regard this practice as a rejection of both them and the preservation of Native society.

Many Aboriginal nations are either entirely matriarchal or have elements of strong female interaction embedded in the culture. There is a belief that women are the protectors and teachers of the culture, especially when it comes to raising children. So when a non-Native woman enters the scene, it can disrupt what some see as the continuing cycle of cultural preservation.

But understanding that, is the talk show host's question still a valid one? True, you go to many functions and social gatherings where the successful Aboriginal intelligentsia gather, and it does seem like the majority of the Native men do sport non-Native spouses. Jordan Wheeler, Native writer for *Sixty Below* and *The Rez* (whose wife, by the way, is a lovely Native woman) blames it on the circles in which "prosperous" Native people are forced to circulate.

Since there are more "successful" White people than Native

people and more "prominent" Native males than females—this is relatively speaking, and I use the terms "successful" and "prominent" loosely—the women a Native male is likely to meet, interact, and develop relationships with will have a mathematical probability of being non-Native. Unfortunate but true.

However, I do seriously doubt this is the only reason. Life is not that simple. Some who like to dabble in amateur (or not so amateur) sociological examination believe there is a deeply subconscious (or maybe not so deep) belief that a non-Native girlfriend is a symbol of success and achievement in both White and Native societies. Or then there's the theory that White women are just easier to find in the dark. I don't know which is the correct answer, or even if there is an answer. One could say that maybe two people just fell in love, but for reasons that I've quoted above, their love has taken on a political taint.

If snuggling with people of no definable Native heritage is a crime, then it is one I am guilty of. Rightly or wrongly, I am a graduate of the "colour-blind school of love." But taking into account the last four girlfriends I have had, I've noticed a disturbing trend developing in my personal life. One that on the surface, may lend credence to the argument.

One of the first serious relationships I ever had was with a Native woman. Sometime afterward I fell in love with a woman who was a half-breed like myself. Then I found myself with a Filipino woman (still technically a visible minority but not Native and not Caucasian). Finally, I spent several years with a White woman. If this trend keeps up, my next girlfriend will either be an albino or an alien.

To the best of my knowledge, none of these relationships were politically or socially motivated. I'm not that bright or ambitious. They just developed as most relationships do. You see each other in a room, make eye contact, you mumble to yourself "oh please God, please," and the rest I'll leave to your imagination.

One older Native woman, a strong proponent of Native men marrying Native women, even verbally chastised me for dating a White girl, urging me to break up with her and start seeing a Native woman she had just recently met. Even though her three daughters had married, had children by, or were simply dating White men, I was the one at fault here. The irony of the situation was not lost on me.

This begs a different angle to the original dating question. Why is it never questioned why successful Native women marry White men (*i.e.* Buffy Sainte-Marie or Tantoo Cardinal)? Granted the ratio is substantially different but still I think it is a valid issue. I even posed that question to the hostess on the radio show. She looked at me blankly for a moment before answering "I don't know. I don't have an answer for that."

And is it only the White culture that's at question here? The issue of the dominant culture absorbing and sublimating the much smaller Aboriginal culture? What about, for sake of argument, a Native and Black combination? There was no noticeable reaction to my relationship with my Filipino girlfriend—in fact, many people jokingly commented that she looked more Native than I did. What about the Asians, both South (the real "Indians") and East? And if you really want to throw a wrench into the works, what about the Sami, the Aboriginal people of Scandinavia, otherwise known as the Laplanders? They all have blonde hair and blue eyes but are recognized as an Indigenous people. I've been claiming to be half Sami, half Ojibway for years.

And does this question only relate to heterosexual couples? What about gay and lesbian relationships? I've never heard of any grief being given or received over an inter-racial relationship in either community. It all gets so confusing.

So I sit here, a single man, afraid to pick up the telephone and call somebody. For, depending on whom I phone, I will no doubt be making a very important and major political statement. And I just want somebody to go to the movies with.

# How Native is Native if You're Native?

Within the growing and diverse Native community, an ongoing ideological battle seems to be raging. One that seems to have become reversed from what it was decades ago. I remember that when I was growing up, the more "Native" you looked—*i.e.* dark skinned with prominent Aboriginal features, the lower you were on the social totem pole (no cultural appropriation of West Coast symbolism intended).

White was "in" and Native people (and, no doubt, many other ethnic cultures) tried to look it, dress it, or act it. Those that didn't were often made fun of. Being dark was no lark. In the Caucasian world, people whose family history included a drop or two of Native blood bent over backwards to keep the scandal a secret. The skeletons in those closets would thrill anthropologists and museums the world over.

These days, it's a completely different ball game. Native is "in." The darker you are, the more you are embraced, the more "Indian" you are thought to be. The lighter your skin, the more difficult it sometimes is to be accepted by your Aboriginal peers (and the non-Native world). White is no longer right. And heaven forbid that those in the dominant culture with some barely remembered ancestor that happened to tickle toes and trade more than some furs and beads with a Native person, should let a conversation slip by without mentioning that at least four of the twenty-four chromosomes in their body don't burn in the summer sun.

But it's often more than simply how you look. It's how you think, act, where you live, and point with your lower lip. Consequently, something more representational of the existing philosophical schism is the difficult question of determining "what makes a Native a Native?" What set of qualifications or characteristics will allow an individual to speak as a Native person, or have an opinion

104

representative of the larger Indigenous population? Sure as hell beats me. But, as sure as there are a hundred websites devoted to "Xena the Warrior Princess," there are a vast number of "experts" in this world eager to tell you what defines a Native and will more than happily tell you whether you fit into that category.

Personally I think it must be great to have all the answers. My ambition in life is to be such an expert. I have done the necessary amount of research. God (or the Creator) knows my bluish-green eyes have allowed me a unique entry into such discussions. Drew Hayden Taylor: Aboriginal Attitude and Attributes Assessor (DHT: AAAA).

One example in the broad spectrum of modern Aboriginal acceptance relates to the world of education. Many Reserves and Native educational organizations are constantly encouraging and extolling the virtues of education to the youth. Yet, there are many individuals in these communities who believe that the more educated you become, the less "Native" you become. They scorn and disdain those who want to or have gone through the conventional educational process. Evidently, scholastic knowledge and learning deprives an individual of their cultural heritage. I must have missed that in the sweat lodge.

Conversations with Elders and traditional teachers have convinced me that this is not a traditional belief or teaching. Many Elders urge and encourage the pursuit of education. In fact, the two worlds of traditional and scholastic education can, and often do, travel the same roads, albeit one on horseback and the other on a vintage 1953 Indian Scout motorcycle. In fact, those that are often wary of formal education are usually locked somewhere between both worlds, they're neither traditional nor particularly well educated. Unfortunately, it is their own insecurity that is being revealed, proving the need for educated Native psychologists.

Another example on the flip-side involves the disquieting story of a Reserve education counselor in a southern Ontario community. Practically every year this person would ask at least one, and who-knows-how-many, off-Reserve students "why should you continue going to university?" She would then strongly hint that this student almost owes it to the community to quit school, saving the Reserve money.

So, if some students on the Reserve are being urged not to go to university, where is all the university-fund money going? This is what's called the I-don't-know-if-I-should-go-to-school-or-stay-home-and-collect-welfare-or-possibly-scratch-out-a-living-telling-students-what-to-do paradox.

I have a column in a Regina newspaper/magazine jokingly called "The Urbane Indian." I was telling this to a Native woman at a meeting and she asked me what urbane meant. I told her it was similar to sophisticated, refined, or knowledgeable. She thought for a moment before responding "I hope I never get like that." Evidently being suave and debonair (or as we say on the Reserve, swave and debone-her) is not a Native characteristic worth having.

There are also those who believe that the more successful you are, the less Native you are. If you have money, toys, a nice house, two accountants, and a vague idea of where the Caribbean is, then you are obviously not one of the Indigenous people. I remember reading an interview with a successful Native prairie businessman who was looked down upon by his brethren because he had made a financial success of his life. And he rationalized it as, "If being Indian means being poor, then I don't necessarily want to be Indian." A harsh statement indicating that he did not think there was any middle ground. I know many successful Aboriginals who are every bit as "Native" as those who still subsist on Kraft dinner and drive 1974 Dodge pickups with multi-coloured doors.

A friend of mine severely criticized another friend because she had made the decision to live in the city while he had moved back to the Reserve. He felt that you could only be Native, or really call yourself an Aboriginal person, within the confines of those artificial borders. Yet he had moved back home in his mid-thirties, having never lived on a Reserve and having grown up in urban environments. I guess he finally and officially considered himself an "Indian."

Taking all of this into consideration, I guess this means the only true "Native" people are uneducated poor people with limited vocabularies that live on the Reserve. Yikes!

As cliché as it may sound, I think everybody has their own unique definition of what being Native means. Very few of us exist in the world our grandparents lived in, where their definition was, no doubt, far from ours. And this definition will no doubt further evolve in the coming millennium. My career as "DHT: AAAA" will have to wait because I don't have all the answers. I don't know the boundaries and the necessary factors for making these decisions. To tell you the truth, I don't even care anymore.

I do know one thing though. Passing judgement on other people isn't a particularly Aboriginal thing to do. I know this because an eagle came to me in my dreams, along with a coyote and a raven; they landed on the tree of peace, smoked a peace pipe, ate a baloney sandwich, played some bingo, and then told me so.

That should shut them up.

# It's Not Easy Speaking a "Bizarro Language"

I was once told that being born Indian in this country is a political act in itself. And in many cases, participating in our culture and even speaking the language are becoming issues in our highly politicized world. Somewhere out west, a little battle took place, with both victors and casualties. It was the latest battle in the war of academic acceptance of Native culture—one trying to prove the legitimacy and equality of Native way of existence in the academic world.

I am a member of the great Anishnawbe nation, or as we are better known to some, the mighty and good-looking Ojibway people. And as a member of this prosperous community, I was surprised and shocked to learn that, according to a certain western university in the midst of Blackfoot territory, my people and I are also speakers of what this bastion-of-academic-freedom refers to as a "bizarro language." I wasn't aware that this was a designated and authentic category used by professional linguists.

As with many things in the Native community, it begins with a relative of mine. A cousin seeking an education out west, the land of supposed opportunity, was aspiring to graduate with honours. And in order to do so, she had to pursue a second language. All fine and dandy. Rather than learn French, or German or Russian, none of which would have any practical usage in her life, she logically opted to study Ojibway, her mother tongue. So far so good.

So, when she first approached her Canadian Studies department with this proposition, they said they would contact the linguistics department and have them write up a test for her to do. First mistake, according to my learned cousin. She objected to this since she had never been taught how to read or write this oral language. Especially since translation of the language was a fairly recent phenomenon.

Scratching their heads at the concept, but acknowledging the logic, the department then told her they would find a qualified Ojibway instructor to test her. Wrong again, my cousin said, since there are numerous dialects ranging from western Quebec to the Manitoba/Saskatchewan border. The dialect she wanted had to come from our Reserve.

By this time, the department was getting a little frustrated and told her that if she could find a certified Ojibway instructor in our community, they would accept her request. Our village, like many Native villages, had such an educated (in academically accepted terms) and accomplished instructor available to administer the test.

Finally, after all the haggling and discussion, and flying home at her own expense, she underwent the testing. She passed with "flying cultures," as any relative of mine would. By this time she was feeling quite good about herself and her struggle. She felt that by getting the test done, she would be paving the way for other Native students to utilize their mother tongues in academia and achieve recognition for it. Unfortunately with youth comes a certain amount of naiveté. It was a wonderful thought though. A thought the university didn't agree with.

During the final meeting with the powers-that-be in that department, she was told, to her face, that because of all the hassles she had caused the department, she was the "last of the 'bizarro languages'" to slip through. The policy has since been changed. The tests now have to be administered for a bona fide language with a written history, so that the linguistics department can test and judge students in "regular" terms. Again, this implies Ojibway and other Indigenous languages are not bona fide and cannot be judged in "regular" terms. It makes me wonder if all Aboriginal languages are viewed as disreputable and illegitimate as the Ojibway tongue by the educational establishment.

Upon reflection, my cousin wonders if she did the right thing. "As far as I am concerned, it would have been easier to do their bogus French test with as much time as I needed and a dictionary rather than have to listen and translate a difficult language." Not much of an option.

Since this wonderful episode in the world of academia, she has informed me that quite a few students who were in the Canadian Studies program at this western university were unable to complete the mandatory second-language requirement but were fluent in an Indigenous language. The irony of Canadian Studies: it doesn't include an Indigenous language. Higher education: an oxymoron.

For obvious reasons my cousin has requested I not mention her name or the exact university she is still attending, for evidently, there are politics aplenty happening. But hats-off to my cousin who is both achieving a higher education and graduating at the top of her "bizarro language 101" class. Unfortunately, she may be the last to do so in this western university in the heart of Blackfoot country.

# The United Church Apology

Yet another case of guilt has forced a major Canadian church to apologize to a Native community for the abuse suffered by Aboriginal children at a church-and government-run Residential School. Last May in Port Alberni, British Columbia, the United Church of Canada apologized to the Nuu-Chah-Nulth people (formerly the Nootka) for what had happened behind those brick walls so many years ago. A simple apology for decades of sexual, emotional, and physical abuse at an institution supposedly run in the name of God.

It was an apology that, understandably, many of the local residents refused to accept. Residents who today are still living with the ramifications of one of the most evil deeds perpetrated in the name of assimilation. The result being high rates of alcoholism, sexual abuse (evidence has shown it is cyclical), suicide and a host of other equally tragic illnesses.

I liken it to putting a simple bandage on a gushing open wound and kissing it for good measure. To quote a cliché, talk is cheap. And when you're talking of hundreds, maybe thousands, of people permanently scared by misguided, and in many cases, seriously sick individuals, it is very cheap. Too cheap.

But in all fairness, I don't want to totally discount the attempts by the United Church to make amends. An apology is a good beginning, but only a beginning. And I hope they see it that way.

Now, there are two ways of handling a difficult situation like this: one based in the Canadian legal system, and the other based in traditional Native beliefs.

Any lawyer or judge would tell you to prosecute or sue the villains in this matter. Numerous charges have been brought against former abusers in the recent past and probably more will be pursued in the future. Canadian jurisprudence dictates punishing the wrongdoers. Fine.

But in many Native communities, it is often thought that the best way to deal with perpetrators of evil and mischief is not so much to punish them—the deed is already done and there is no point in trying to change what has already happened—but instead, to provide restitution to the victims for those misdeeds. Healing the damage in the victim, in many cases, is more important than damning the offender. There are thousands of people out there still feeling the ramifications of what happened in those schools, some in serious need of counseling, healing and other forms of assistance.

If both the Church and government are so interested in making amends, perhaps they should consider doing something a little more positive to take care of the problem their dark schools created. Let's see them throw some money or resources to these people along with their apology. Using another cliché, actions speak louder than words.

Recently I visited Pelican Lake in northwestern Ontario. I was there to assist a camera crew from TV Ontario document a healing-and-wellness conference for former students of the Pelican Lake Residential School. The odd and special thing about this particular conference is that it had support, both financially and spiritually, from the Anglican Church of Canada, the former supervisor of the school.

This church had seen the errors of its ways and was attempting to right the wrongs. It's a first step, a beginning. Let's see where things go from here.

# The Plight of the Unemployed

It's supposed to be a good thing that the national unemployment rate is hovering somewhere around nine percent or so. Unless, of course, you're one of those nine percent. And I am. Several months ago I resigned from my job as the Artistic Director of Native Earth Performing Arts, an Aboriginal theatre company. Since then, I've been faithfully checking out all the newspaper want ads and unfortunately, there haven't exactly been a lot of job listings for Native Artistic Directors. There must be a glut in the market or something.

So what's a poor humble ex-A.D. to do in his spare time when he has time to kill and no money to spend? An interesting question. One that I've been examining lately in some detail. For instance, perhaps I could just do the noble starving-artist thing. You know, just hang out drinking wine on the Left Bank. I guess we would be talking the left bank of Lake Ontario, instead of the river Seine in Paris. Somehow the romance seems to get lost in the translation. And I'm not sure the Seine has a wind-chill factor of minus ten degrees Celsius.

How about... becoming a squeegee kid? It's a growing industry. Then again, I don't have the right kind of hair. Besides, there are ethics involved. I don't even clean my own windows, let alone a total stranger's.

I could write the great Canadian Aboriginal Novel! Picture it, a touching and romantic story taking place during a time of war and conflict, specifically the Oka Crisis. It's the tale of a wounded Warrior in a hospital in Montreal, being tenderly looked after by a French-Canadian nurse. It would be called... The Mohawk Patient. On second thought, sounds a bit derivative.

I could devote all my spare time to selfless causes of charity and good will, in an effort to make this world a much better place for me and all its people. Now what would that involve? No more

113

meat—we can't oppress the animals now, can we? To help save the forests, I'd have to cut down on the amount of paper I use to write my works of art—oh great, just what a playwright needs!

What else? Of course my air conditioner would have to go, those annoying fluorocarbons mucking up the atmosphere and all. It's Fall right now, I can live with that. One question though: are latex condoms biodegradable, or better yet, recyclable? Never mind, I don't want to even think about it.

As a last resort, I could go into politics. An ex-playwright was elected President of Czechoslovakia (and now the Czech Republic) several years ago. Never mind, there's enough tragedy happening in politics as it is. You can't even count on Harris's "Workfare"—if he had that up and running properly, I could be enjoying a flourishing career as a hall monitor in Scarborough.

But that would require that I be on welfare first, and most of the provinces have really tightened the applicability requirements for social assistance in recent years. And since my people have only been here for the last 40,000 years, I just might not be eligible.

# It's Election Time

Ah yes, can you smell it in the air? It's springtime, and a young Canadian's fancy turns to thoughts of love, barbecues and federal elections. Now that our fearless leader, Jean Chretien, has called an election, all of us loyal Canadians will soon be trudging off through the streets to cast our democratic ballot.

And the theme of this year's election? A simple six-syllable word that puts the fear of God, or the electorate into the candidate's heart. That word? Accountability. Say it with me. Accountability. If you can say it, spell it, and understand it, things could get exciting this year.

Remember George Bush, the former *grand fromage* from below-the-border and his infamous promise? "Read my lips: No new taxes." That came back to haunt him like drinking the water in Mexico. Our own beloved Sheila Copps made a nasty little boo-boo herself with her vow to resign if the G.S.T. wasn't scrapped. Well, God bless her, when the accountability issue was brought up, she actually did. Of course, she's back now but how can you hate somebody who's dream is to give every single person in the country a Canadian flag? Remember the days when politicians used to promise "a car in every garage and a chicken in every pot?" Now it's just flags. Talk about cutbacks.

And speaking of the G.S.T., can we mention that word to Chretien without him breaking out into a cold, cold sweat? "What G.S.T.?" "I promised what?" Kind of sounds like the things you find yourself promising on a first date, doesn't it?

And let's not forget that court case in B.C. where a private citizen is suing the Provincial Government for not keeping its election promises. Is this the right thing to do? I don't know. I never took an ethics or political science course in school.

So, in honour of the election of 1997, I want to propose a new political game that everyone can play. It's a lottery of sorts. You, the voter, chose three election promises and record them with an independent agency set up for just such a purpose. Then, just before the next election, the person who has correctly chosen the highest number of unfulfilled promises wins! And as they say, to the victor goes the spoils: the prize would be a complete lifetime exemption from the G.S.T. In theatre, we call this a metaphor. One dripping with irony, I might add.

I think this little game should be called the Liberal Liars' Lottery, or LLL, or $L^3$. You can also play this with the NDP, the Reform Party, the P.C. Party, and any other political party, but the alliteration may not work as well.

I know I probably sound very cynical and skeptical, but one can't help remembering that eighty years ago the Federal Government instituted this little thing called the Income Tax, saying it was only a temporary measure to help finance World War I. Well, didn't we win that war? A long time ago?

# STRAIGHT FROM THE ART
## (MOVIES, PLAYS, AND BOOKS, OH MY!)

# James Owl or Grey Bond

In the woods just north of Montreal, near the town of Magog, a multimillion-dollar movie has just completed shooting. The lead actor: television and film star Pierce Brosnan. The plot: a tale of stolen identities, disguises and mystery, of bedding numerous women and then disappearing into the sunset, of dangerous situations and daring-do in remote lands. Quite simply, a story no one would believe in a million years.

Contrary to the way it sounds, it's not the next James Bond film. Instead, it's the story of one of the greatest impersonators, or wannabe icons, if you prefer, to ever grace our beloved country. The movie, *Grey Owl*, tells the story of Archie Belaney: a turn-of-the-century English boy who, at the age of eighteen, decides to run off to Canada to be an Indian. As it's said, some are born to greatness or Aboriginal heritage, others have it thrust upon them (or take it themselves).

Our hero Archie starts off learning the fine art of trapping and bush survival up Temegami way where he received his name, Grey Owl. He then spent some time in Quebec, and later finished his years in Saskatchewan where he died at the age of fifty.

During the thirty-odd years he spent in Canada, he married at least three times, was wounded as a sniper in World War I (he enlisted to avoid a warrant for his arrest in Canada), wrote several books under the name Grey Owl, and became quite the celebrated "Aboriginal" author and conservationist. Altogether, it sounds like the makings for an interesting Hollywood film. Especially one directed by Sir Richard Attenborough, the idealistic scientist in *Jurassic Park* and also the director of *Ghandi*.

If one tries hard enough, one can already envision scenes from the movie. Pierce Brosnan appears out of the bush fresh from his trap-line, dressed in moccasins and braids; he notices a beautiful young Native maid (maybe it's Pocahontas, I'm sure James Bond has used the name John Smith many times) standing by a canoe. He approaches her carrying his bundle of freshly prepared fur, and she asks who he is. He answers with his clipped British accent, "The name's Owl. Grey Owl. And I like my beaver shaken, not stirred."

Okay, so maybe it doesn't happen that way. But according to a source of mine that worked on the set, a lot of interesting things did happen during the production. For instance, Grey Owl was famous for adopting young beavers and raising them. Well, the beaver wranglers (that's what the people who train beavers are called) lost the beaver. It escaped. No doubt in a very James Bondish manner, using a jet-pack made out of poplar twigs. I think they had to bring in a stunt beaver to finish the shoot.

Already worried about the politically dubious nature of a film glorifying such a wanton cultural appropriator, the Native people who worked on the film renamed the costume department (because the traditional dancers do not wear "costumes!") to a more correct term: the regalia department. As a result, the craft services department, which provides the cast and crew with munchies during the actual shoot, was renamed "Kraft services" and specialized in macaroni and cheese, or macaroni with tomatoes.

And, I'm sorry to report, there are unconfirmed accounts concerning the inability of a certain super-spy to dance a decent intertribal. In fact, a particular P.B. had to receive special tutoring in how to keep the rhythm of the drum in an attempt to dance believably. And even then, I'm told, the results were questionable. He kept dancing with an accent.

And as for the movie, because of copyright laws and such, the drum group hired for the Powwow scene was reluctant to use or record authentic drum songs. Instead, to their credit, they wrote a specific theme song for the production which they call the Grey Owl Intertribal. Soon to be heard at a Powwow near you.

But the serious irony of the whole story behind Grey Owl, his legend, and this movie is that the name Grey Owl is actually a translation of the Ojibway title given to him in Temegami, Ontario: *Wah-Sha-Quon-Asin*. The literal rendering of that phrase for this chameleon-of-a-man comes across as He-Who-Flies-By-Night. I think that says it all.

And with that, the whole set explodes with a fiery bang as our hero, known as "Owl, Grey Owl," shoots his way through the forest only to appear at Casino Rama playing baccarat with a glass of Labatt's 50, shaken, not stirred. With Buffy Sainte-Marie singing the theme song. It works for me.

# Colour Television? Where's the Colour?!

If you're a television watcher, then you've noticed the new television season has arrived with all the usual fanfare we've come to expect. CBC, CTV, Global, and all the rest have proudly thrust into our faces all the new shows of the Fall. But as a Native person watching Canadian television, I have noticed a single, uncomfortable fact that prevents me from celebrating this national pastime. Is it my imagination, or does television seem a little bland—pigment-wise, I mean?

In seasons past, there were shows like *The Rez*—the bastard child of W.P. Kinsella's questionable short stories—*North of Sixty*—the "what will we do to Tina Keeper this week" show—and *All My Relations*—a current affairs, "who's doing what, when, where, and to whom" type show. In the more distant past there were shows like *Spirit Bay*, a Native children's view of innocent life on the Reserve, and *The Beachcombers* which asked the important question: "can a chubby Indian find happiness and success in small town British Columbia." Of course this was all before the Reform Party.

But this season there seems to be a noticeable lack of shows with Aboriginal actors and themes. I've learned to expect that from CTV, and even Global, but CBC? Part of the networks' mandate is to help define and represent the multicultural population of Canada. Has it suddenly decided that there are no more Native people in Canada worth representing? I hope not, because that sure will be a shock to all my relatives back home in Central Ontario.

So what do we have to look forward to this TV season? Not much it seems. In case you haven't noticed, those Native-theme shows have all been cancelled. *North of Sixty* will wrap up all its loose ends in a two-hour made-for-TV movie airing sometime this winter. And the epic mini-series, *Big Bear*, is set to be broadcast sometime later in the season. That's it. Several tens of thousands of prime time hours and we get, maybe, six. Boy, a lot must have happened in Canada and at the CBC in the last year to practically wipe us off primetime.

So that begs the question "what's left?" Where can some of the issues being faced by Native Canadians be explored and broadcast to Canada? *Traders*? I doubt it. I don't know many Native stockbrokers, though the thought of letting one loose to wreak havoc on Daisohwa stocks and various mining operations does present interesting dramatic possibilities. *Due South*? Unfortunately, the shared history of Mounties and Natives doesn't lend itself to light comedydrama. What about that new show *Da Vinci's Inquest*? If memory serves correctly, he's a coroner. I don't even want to go there.

What's even more peculiar, CBC's licence is coming up for renewal in the new year. It should be worried about this imbalance. Yet there seems to be more interest from the corporation in representing a substantially insignificant minority in Canada than its original inhabitants. I am speaking of comedians. This minority gets to carry such shows like, *Sketchcom*, *This Hour Has 22 Minutes*, *Comics*, *Air Farce*, just to name a few. I know far more Native people than comedians. Don't you think something is wrong here?

I remember when *Dances With Wolves*, *Dry Lips Oughta Move to Kapuskasing*, and *North of Sixty* came out, many people were claiming Native people were just the latest "flavour of the month." I guess that means now we're just an aftertaste. I bet the over one million people in Canada who claim some form of Aboriginal ancestry will find that interesting. Does this mean I'll have to move to Riverdale to be represented on Canadian television?

But lest I leave you with no hope, Television Northern Canada has brought an application before the CRTC, Canada's broadcast licenser. They are proposing something quite exciting: a whole channel specifically devoted to, produced by, and set up for the Aboriginal people of Canada. Before you know it, we'll all be watching *Touched by an Anglo*.

123

# Colour of the Month

It wasn't that long ago, somewhere around 1990 I believe, that Native people had yet another "colourful" (pun intended) euphemism thrust upon them. Because of the success of movies like *Dances With Wolves*, *Powwow Highway*, and *Last of the Mohicans*, and plays like *The Rez Sisters* and *Dry Lips Oughta Move to Kapuskasing*, Aboriginal people were being classified as the "flavour of the month." It seemed everybody wanted to write stories about Native people.

Well, that was about seven years ago, and it has turned into a very long month. Perhaps they were talking about that proverbial "month of Sundays"? During that long and culturally enriched period of time, there were plenty of other movies released with Native themes at their heart. I give you *Geronimo*, *Dance Me Outside*, *Dead Man*, *Thunderheart*, *The Indian in the Cupboard*, just to mention a few.

Both of the last two movies star the once-fine actor Tom Berenger (remember him in *The Big Chill* and *Platoon*?), and have him battling against Indians. *Last of the Dog Men*, a little-seen film shot in Banff, has the modern-day Berenger accidentally discovering a lost and untouched tribe of Cheyenne, still living a traditional life in the foothills of the Rockies. The other film, a violent urban drama called *The Substitute*, has him coming up against old Wind-In-His-Hair himself, Rodney A. Grant, as a Seminole drug smuggler in Florida. What about combining both Berenger films into a single tale about a lost tribe of Indian drug smugglers?

Anyway, I always had confidence that the "flavour of the month" moniker would be a misnomer. I knew that only the tip of the iceberg had been discovered when it came to telling Native stories, however improbable those stories might be.

But I must admit that I was getting worried. It seems like the

124

month that started all those years ago was over. It appeared the movie going public was becoming more interested in stories exploring another clan-oriented people: the Scots. Witness the success of 1995's *Rob Roy*, the several Academy Awards for *Braveheart*, and all the buzz surrounding last year's smash movie, *Trainspotting*, a story about a lost generation of drug users. Maybe they and the gang from *Last of the Dog Men* and *The Substitute* should get together.

Then I began to think that maybe I was a little premature. It wasn't the Scots, it was the Irish that were now in vogue. For the last few years, there seemed to be a growing number of top-quality Irish movies: *My Left Foot, In the Name of the Father, The Secret of Roan Inish, Michael Collins, The Commitments*, etc.

Feeling just a little threatened, I went to the movie section of my local newspaper, just to make sure. My heart was breaking. There wasn't an Indian to be seen at either the Cineplex or Famous Players. Just movies about angels, dogs and Martians. Was the cinematic interest in us Indians over? It could have been just an off day.

Then my eye caught the ad for another movie playing near-by. A critically acclaimed film called *Some Mother's Son*. And where does it takes place? In Ireland. I was right.

No more *Indian in the Cupboard*. Now it's the *Leprechaun in the Sock Drawer*.

# My Name Soars Like An Eagle

In a magazine (that shall remain nameless) specializing in new ways of looking at life, there's an ad for a "spiritual development" workshop called "Cry for A Vision." "Join us for four and a half days on the land as we traverse the shadow and retrieve the light. Ceremonies and teachings are based on ancient shamanic wheels and keys. Set your intent for the coming year and dance it awake." The last names of the two dancing workshop leaders are Crystal Light Warrior and Butterfly Dreamer.

I must say that, as a First Nations person, reading stuff like this makes me wish we had colourful names like that on our Reserve. I'm almost ashamed to say they sound a hell of a lot more interesting than Taylor, Jacobs or Knott.

With the growing popularity of the New Age and other movements sympathetic to the Native cause, taking on Aboriginal names and personae seems to be an ongoing and ever-popular hobby among people searching for a new way of looking at life. Pseudo-Indian names currently abound and prosper on the shelves of most bookstores with sizable sections for books of a more metaphysical nature. It seems odd but fitting that after five hundred years of taking our land, language, culture and ways of life, these people are now reduced to taking our names. Or what they think are our names. A casual perusal of titles in a bookstore specializing in New Age literature provides a cornucopia of pseudo-traditional Native author names. Ones that make you wonder "Who the hell are these people and why do they feel the need to mix and match various animal and nature words randomly?"

Personally, I know very few people of Native ancestry who feel the need to write self-help books promising universal peace and a cosmic path to follow. It isn't exactly kosher. Even if they did, they probably wouldn't do it under pseudonyms that sound like Nintendo games—Crystal Light Warrior?

I think you definitely have to be White with far too much time on your hands to come up with colourful names like that today. And a closer examination of these New Age-coloured Native names reveals some interesting characteristics. First of all, most of them usually have one of four specific references in them: wind, fire, feather, and wolf (a bear or deer can be substituted with proper authorization). Secondly, they're all in English. And thirdly, they're all beautiful examples of nature/animals-turning-into-human metaphors.

Even in this age of political correctness, these prepetrators of cultural appropriation still seem to be getting all the breaks. And if you actually read the author biographies in some of these books, you'll notice how vague and non-exact the descriptions of the people behind these expressive names are, probably on purpose. They include lines like this: "Hairy Turtle Sneezing lives in the deepest, darkest part of the woods where he communes regularly with nature when not astral projecting."

One cannot help but get the impression that the only Native people most of these writers know are in the *Dances With Wolves* video tape they keep perpetually cued in the VCR. Names such as Blackwolf, Gary Buffalo Horn Man, Sherry Fire Dancer, White Deer of Autumn, and, my personal favourite, Summer Rain with her faithful Indian companion, No-Eyes, described as "her beloved Indian Shaman Teacher" (I kid you not!), are just a cross section.

Mysticism and the belief in a world outside the physical one we inhabit is a strong and honoured belief among most Aboriginals, but I must have been astral projecting the day they gave out beloved Indian Shaman teachers. But, fortunately, my birthday's coming up. Besides, I'm starting to see how this works. My girlfriend is studying for her Master in Education; that makes her a teacher, not to mention my beloved teacher. She's also Mohawk. So she's a beloved Indian teacher. Luckily she has some Irish blood—so in total, I guess she's my beloved Indian Shamus Teacher. It seems to lose something in the translation.

And the authors you read about on the backs of these New Age book jackets are just the lucky ones with decent publicists. Out there, on the Powwow grounds, in the craft shops, and hanging out at the Friendship Centres, are masses of uniquely named individuals, keeping low profiles, and generally hanging out looking for spiritual guidance and, if possible, an even better-sounding Indigenous name.

Of course, the Aboriginal world isn't the only one that induces cultural envy. I've seen people of many different cultures explore and dabble in the exotic elements of a variety of cultures other than their own. I, for one, have been known to wear Italian leather, eat a lot of Thai food, and dare I say, wear cowboy boots. But, to the best of my knowledge, my name has always been Drew Hayden Taylor.

Traditionally, those who were given a special "Indian" name were usually required to use it on special occasions only; it was a personal, private name. Putting it on business cards seems to defeat that purpose. I know many Native people who have a traditional name. Sharing it with somebody is a sign of great respect. Putting it on a book cover to make money is not.

Again, different culture, different priorities. Let us not forget that in some Native communities "colourful" family names are frequently used. I've known some Whiteducks, Many Grey Horses, New Breasts, Tailfeathers, and the odd Goodstriker, to name just a few. But somehow, their attitude toward their last names is a little less esoteric and a little more natural. There isn't any "traversing shadow and retrieving the light" involved. Maybe after the occasional beer, but not much.

Another point, traditionally, is that glancing through books dealing with Aboriginal history provides an interesting, if not downright ironic, twist. A simple assessment of authentic Aboriginal names of the past includes such mystical and beautiful titles as Sitting Bull, Crazy Horse, Dull Knife, Bloody Knife, Roman Nose, Old Man Afraid Of His Horses, Big Foot, Black Kettle, Crow Dog, Gall, Rough Feather, Wild Hog, Hairy Bear, Lame Deer, Leg-In-The-Water, Low Dog, and Stumbling Bear, to name just a few. But would you buy a self-help book from Bloody Knife?

In all fairness, I believe people should be allowed to do whatever they want. So, maybe, as a point, I should write my own book. L. Ron Hubbard was once quoted as saying something like: if you want to be rich someday, start your own religion. I can do that. But Drew Hayden Taylor does not exactly exude Aboriginal confidence and ancient Shamanic wisdom. I must concoct one of these awe-inspiring names.

My book will be called *Spiritual Enlightenment in the New Millennium—How To Receive Completion of your Spirit's Journey Through The Adoption of Caucasian/Christian Names*. It will be written by me, Spread Eagle, and my girlfriend, Eager Beaver. I'm ready for Oprah (which spelled backwards is Harpo).

# The Good, the Bad, and the "Abies"

It's late spring and I once again find myself winging my way west in hopes of having fun, meeting interesting people, finding out why the Reform Party of Canada is so popular, and seeing the latest and greatest in what's happening in the Aboriginal film community. Yes, it's my annual pilgrimage to the Dreamspeakers Aboriginal Film Festival. And, it was, as always, eventful with some unusual, wonderful, and not so wonderful surprises. Much like life.

In its seventh year, Dreamspeakers offers Edmonton, and the Native filmmakers of Canada (and America, with the occasional remarkable film from New Zealand and Australia thrown in) the opportunity to enjoy and celebrate the fabulous growth in Aboriginal film production. It also provides the occasion to rub shoulders with the famous, the hoping-to-be-famous, the not-quite-as-famous-as-they-think, and the ever-present blue-eyed Aboriginal playwrights.

This year's adventures began, naturally, at the beginning, on the plane heading out to Edmonton. I was calmly eating what appears to be a microwaved, reconstituted, near-perfect imitation of a chicken dinner when the fire alarm inside the plane goes off. At thirty-five thousand feet. What does one do in a situation like this, other than scream? Like the vast majority of the passengers, I did not pay any attention to the flight attendants as they told us what to do in an emergency situation. I briefly envisioned a note of my limited attention span being chipped into my tombstone. Like my mother always said, I should pay attention more often.

Luckily, the alarm soon ceased as several flight attendants quickly ran in a several directions. It wasn't long before the captain's voice came on the air, telling us that someone had been smoking in the bathroom and that this was a federal offense endangering our lives. But calm was now restored. Until we landed. After pulling up to the gate, the captain's voice was heard again, telling us that we would not be docking until the R.C.M.P. boarded the plane to "escort" the gentleman with the uncontrollable addiction off the plane. Pretty soon, two officers did indeed board the plane, located a gentleman up near the front of the plane where everybody could see the rebel, and took him away. Last I heard, as part of his community-service sentence, he is now on a good-will tour of Native communities, promoting the benefits of Residential Schools. That'll teach him.

An interesting beginning to what turned out to be a fun festival. The night of the Aboriginal Film Awards, the "Abies," proved to be a mixed blessing for the organizers. Many of the invited and nominated artists and celebrities managed to make it to the awards, including such luminaries as Wes Studi (*Last of the Mohicans, Geronimo, Deep Rising*), Michael Horse (*Twin Peaks, X-Files, North of Sixty*), and Irene Bedard (*Pocahontas, Lakota Woman*).

Wes, who usually plays dark and ominous characters, was always quick with a smile, and turned out to be a dapper dresser. Michael and I traded one-liners all weekend. His best idea for a Native television show: *Touched by an Anglo*. Mine: *Hudson's Baywatch*. Irene was lovely, though very tiny. I quickly surmised that I could eat her body weight in a day.

Unfortunately, the awards night was plagued by several notable no-shows, including the usually reliable Gary Farmer, Rodney Grant, and Dakota House. This left gaps in the show that had to be quickly re-jigged to show no appreciable damage. Also, for some strange reason, only one of the festival's board members managed to find the time to attend the most important night of the organization's existence. What was especially disappointing was the fact that the two board members who were supposed to present Wes Studi with a star blanket, as had been advertised and promoted, failed to show, forcing the organizers to—luckily—locate and present the easy-going actor with an eagle feather. Again, no appreciable damage other than some frustrated words backstage.

The good news of the festival, like in past festivals, was the unusual opportunities and events, both planned and unplanned, that materialize out of the film fair. The definite highlight for me was a private and personal concert for Pura Fe, Jimmy Herman, and three

131

others, including myself, by a new women's *a cappella* group, consisting of mostly Cree women. Called Asani which means rock in Cree, they sung a fabulous doo-wop version of a Murray Porter song—they called it "1492: Who Found Who"—as well as a hilarious Aboriginal version of Roberta Flack's "Killing Me Softly With His Song." Except in Asani's version, it's about looking for a man who makes the perfect fried bread. They call it "Killing Me Softly with Cholesterol." Evidently they judge a man by the size of his bannock. As long as it's not too hard.

Other highlights included a jam session at C-Weeds, including Hawk and Eagle, Wes Studi on bass, and Pura Fe on vocals. Try to envision it, but trust me it was better than you can imagine.

And then there was watching Irene Bedard and Jennifer Podemski as role models in a local non-alcohol dance club for Native youth, being entertained in a special show by a local hip hop/dance/rap group. You could see that Irene and Jennifer were blown away by what these young people were doing. It was an honour to be there.

Dreamspeakers 1998. At least at this film festival, nobody mentioned anything about *Godzilla* or *The Horse Whisperer*. Okay, one person made a bad joke about a new movie he was working on called *The Moose Whisperer*. But I promised not to repeat it.

# The Theatre Files: The Money is Out There

Although it has been said many times before, and in many different ways, the Federal Government's current war against the tobacco companies has the potential to cost the entertainment and sports industries plenty. And in more ways than one. While this is early on in the battle, there is the potential for some very serious and bizarre side effects.

As Artistic Director of a small Native theatre company, and a non-profit one at that, a large part of my responsibilities includes the never-ending, beating-of-the-bushes for funding, grants, and endorsements to help feed, clothe, and house our darling, growing brood of actors, directors, stage managers, designers, and all the other production staff we call our family. We love them and want to take care of them.

But in recent years, the constant cut backs in municipal, provincial, and federal monies allocated to the arts has limited our ability to provide the necessities of life for our growing family. Add to that the sudden attack on the tobacco industry that has always been sympathetic to our cause (albeit for reasons of its own), and we're left in a bit of a pickle. It's the equivalent of your Mom feeding you only half a sandwich, and then telling you that you can't grab a bite at McDonald's.

This became more apparent when we received a much-needed grant from one of the major tobacco organizations to sponsor one of next season's main-stage productions. We were very delighted that our actors wouldn't have to put off those long-awaited operations until we read the line "… the Tobacco Act (Bill C-71), which may impact on our ability to fulfil our undertaking to sponsor numerous Canadian arts, endeavors, possibly including yours. Please understand that our grant as outlined herein may be subject to this legislation, which we have no control of." Evidence that the Federal

Government had been there, peeing in our Rice Crispies.

It's been said that Nature abhors a vacuum. I believe people will still want to write, act in, and see plays, regardless of how much money is available to produce this noble art, and there are only so many one-person plays on a totally black set with a single light-bulb for atmosphere that the audience will tolerate. People and theatre companies will find a way to finance their productions.

As a consequence, I am forced into a position of finding, shall we say, alternative sources of funding. I am pursuing avenues that, until recently, would never have occurred me, or my peers. Thus, my company, Native Earth Performing Arts, and I find we are weighing ethical and moral dilemmas that result from the search for money. Ones that far outweigh the tobacco issue.

For instance, as a Native theatre company, there would be certain problems should we consider approaching Labatt, Molson, Seagram, or any number of liquor organizations. An understandable dilemma, but when you reach your second or third cash-flow problem in a season, such moral difficulties begin to carry less weight. Always remember, there's nothing scarier than hungry costume designers. I myself wouldn't have a problem taking money from these organizations; I am delighted that they would be interested in putting money back into the Native community, but unlike most other theatre companies, Native Earth must answer and be responsible to its community. Again, a pickle. Feed your actors, or be sensitive to the concerns of the community.

I was once approached by an intermediary acting on behalf of some cigarette smugglers, back when there was still some profit in it. They were interested in putting some money back into the community. Would Native Earth like to be a beneficiary of this effort? My beloved General Manager shrugged for a moment, simply saying "all money has blood on it, if you follow it back far enough. Sure, we'll take it." She then added quickly, "as long as they're not drug smugglers." I assured her they weren't. But as things turned out, we never heard from them again anyway.

Last year somebody who shall remain nameless approached me about a rather unconventional sponsor. I was asked if I would have a problem taking a donation/grant/sponsorship from a strip club. Again, an interesting dilemma. Should we, as a socially respon-

134

sible theatre company take money from a business that has been accused of exploiting and degrading women? Then, as I hear grumbling coming from the stomachs of several stage managers, I can't help but think that many of these women (and men I might add) make more in a week than I or the average stage manager make in a month. Personally, I could handle that kind of exploitation.

I could also do the Mother Teresa route. This paragon of virtue has rubbed shoulders with such questionable luminaries as the Duvaliers (formally of Haiti), Charles Keating (currently under the hospitality of the American penal system), and the Hoxhas (former rulers of Albania). All in the pursuit of raising money to fund her orphanage in India. Would I have brunch with Kadaffi to finance the first all-Native production of *Henry V*? Good question. I don't know.

One could always imitate little league baseball, I suppose. You've seen kids playing on baseball diamonds across North America, all wearing shirts listing the team sponsor on the back. Picture a production of *Chorus Line* with all the dancers wearing Petro-Canada jackets (not that I have anything against PetroCanada). Or *Julius Caesar* with togas that are courtesy of Honest Ed's (again, not that I have anything against Honest Ed's). But in this changing economic environment, anything is possible.

For a brief moment I also thought about stealing an idea from the film industry. The concept of product placement: for a small investment fee, using a particular company's product in the actual show. Putting a strategically placed can of Coke on the stage of *The Glass Menagerie*. Having Willy Loman in *Death of a Salesman* actually sell something onstage, like Second Cup coffee, the logo plastered all over his briefcase and car. How about eating a Pizza Pizza pizza during *A Long Day's Journey into Night*. Then again, maybe it wouldn't work. Please keep in mind these are the ravings of a desperate Artistic Director. I have many dependents to feed.

The last image I would like to leave you with is from the movie *Rocky*. Remember him walking into the ring for that crucial fight with Apollo Creed at the end of the movie? On the back of his robe was a small advertisement for a meat-packing plant. His brother-in-law, Pauly, got 2,000 dollars for placing it there.

Oh my God, will we be reduced to that?

# What's In a Name?

As an artist, I was stunned to find myself dealing with repercussions from my exposure to one of the few remaining legitimate prejudices, not only existing but flourishing, in most parts of Canada. And it is a most "Canadian" intolerance. No, it has nothing to do with the fact I'm Native. Nor does it have anything to do with me eating meat or not caring much for the game of hockey. I am referring to a simple, though personally devastating, geographical bigotry. I wrote a play with the word "Toronto" in it. That's right, hate me. I'm getting used to it.

Several years ago I authored a play titled *Toronto at Dreamer's Rock*. It was very successful, winning the Chalmer's Playwright Award, which I almost lost in a bar later that night, but that's a completely different story. This play has since had fifteen professional productions in various parts of Canada and has been published in book form. It's even been translated into German! And the ironic thing is, it has absolutely nothing to do with the City of Toronto.

The word "Toronto" is actually an Iroquois word meaning a gathering or meeting place. I was using that concept in the title. It's called a metaphor. We writers use a lot of them. But recently, I have begun to regret having utilized that metaphor, and the word that represents the founding of Canada's largest city.

I will give you an example why. In the mid-90s, *Toronto at Dreamer's Rock* was produced by theatre companies in both Edmonton and Regina. Both organizations asked me, quite timidly, if they could call the play, simply, *Dreamer's Rock*. Curious, I asked why and was informed that a lot of people out west don't like the word, city, or concept of "Toronto." People wouldn't come and see the play.

At first I thought they meant western Canada didn't like gath-

136

ering or meeting places which I thought was quite odd because I didn't find Saskatchewanians or Albertans to be a solitary bunch. I've seen them gathering and meeting. It was then that I was informed of this geographical racism. It seems Toronto and its inhabitants have become the domestic Americans of Canada. Nobody outside of a certain distance of the city wants anything to do with Torontonians, or any references to them.

I tried to tell these companies that the play has practically nothing to do with the actual city of Toronto. In fact, its about three sixteen-year-old Native boys on the top of a rock outcropping located on Manitoulin Island in northern central Ontario. A long way, both in distance and reality, from the city of Toronto. Having read and produced the play, the producers knew that, but they still felt a name change to be somewhat of a necessity. Evidently the name has certain unpleasant connotations that just cannot be ignored.

Trying to understand this, I tried to remember if *A Streetcar Named Desire* had an actual streetcar named "desire" in the text. I don't believe so. Again, it's probably one of those pesky metaphor things. But I guess not too many people really hate streetcars, so it's a moot point. In the end, I did not end up allowing these two companies to change the name.

However, the play was produced in Vancouver last year and the audiences have been, shall we say, quite modest despite a wonderful and expensive advertising campaign. Now, I am not just an irate playwright looking for excuses, I assure you. Although I have had less successful shows before, and may again in the future (but let's hope not), this particular show has proven itself, and the Vancouver production was quite superior. But the Artistic Director of the company, and many of her professional theatre staff, after a serious discussion and market research, blame the limited audience interest on the simple fact that very few people in Vancouver want to see a show with the name "Toronto" in the title. "The meeting or gathering place" is not living up to its name.

And to make the issue more complicated, Carousel Theatre plans to take the play out on a four-month national tour starting in February. While this was in negotiations, I had been strongly urged by the powers that be, though in a very friendly and considerate manner, to consider cutting the title down to, again, simply *Dreamer's*

*Rock.*

But I reasoned, if I do that, I could be opening up the flood gates. What if there are people out there who don't like dreams or dreamers? Does it become just *At Rock*? And what if those same people have had their hearts broken by a geologist, or have lent money to a rock star, never to see him or her or the money again. I am out of a title, except maybe for the "at."

You would think that people will judge the show, not the title, or, more accurately, a single word consisting of seven letters within the title.

It is the irony of the situation that actually infuriates me. People are totally free to dislike as many cities as they want, but as I said before, "Toronto" is actually an Aboriginal word, and we Native people should be proud of it. Granted, it may not have the fine gentrified names of cities like Edmonton, Vancouver, Regina, and Victoria have.

*Vancouver at Dreamer's Rock?*

I don't see it.

# How to Make Love to an Aboriginal Without Sexually Appropriating Him or Her

It wasn't too long ago when Lee Maracle, the well-known Native-writer-turned-actress, and I were having a lively conversation at a downtown watering hole. The subject at hand: the exciting growth and expansion of Native literature, something we both have a familiarity with. In recent years, there have been many inroads made and directions explored by Native writers hitherto unseen; we have produced biographies, comic adventures, dramatic novels, searing political attacks, and a plethora of theatrical plays.

But we also noted that there were still a few avenues of expression that had not been, as yet, tested. Erotica, for some unknown reason, sprang to our minds.

Pooling our experiences, we both had come across a few poems and some theatre that bordered on the erotic, but other than those few samples, the pickings were pretty lean in that department. And knowing that Nature hates a vacuum (not to mention two writers in search of a good idea), we toyed with the idea of co-editing a book of native erotica (not to be confused with Native "neurotica" of course). Between the two of us we knew we could put together the finest samples of literary love Native writers had to offer; page upon page of pounding pulses, sweaty skin, heaving bosoms... why should White people have all the fun?

The closest I had ever come to the concept of Native erotica was a book of so-called erotic legends I had read as a teenager. Called *Tales from the Smokehouse*, it featured a series of amorous adventures with such characters as Big Arrow, and was narrated by men in a sweat lodge. Compiled and written by a White writer, some of the tales had a decidedly contemporary setting and feel. The fact that one of the stories takes place in Montreal during Expo '67 leaves me to doubt the collection's authenticity.

The more we talked about our little project, the more excited we became. First we had to discuss what the parameters of the collection would be. Specifically, how would we define Native erotica? What separates our erotica from other types of erotica? My argument was the real difference between the two was that in Native erotica there are no tan lines.

However, the former journalist in me saw the need to research this properly before the writing could take place. Some have argued that one type of Native erotica (stories about Natives, not by Natives) is already alive and well, and available at your local bookstore. Much like *Tales from the Smokehouse*, non-Native writers have tapped into the lust-filled Aboriginal angle long before Lee and I came up with our hot-and-heavy little idea.

Visit the historical romance department of any substantial bookstore, and you'll see an amazing selection of literature that features a magnificent Native man (well muscled, dressed in a taut, laced-buckskin breech cloth, and always leaning at a forty-five-degree angle) with a mane-and breast-blessed woman (almost always fiery, independent, and White) that is willing to loosen the ties that bind, if you know what I mean.

Here is a random sampling of what's available:

*Wild Thunder by Cassie Edwards*

*"You have come to see the horses," Strong Wolf said. Suddenly, alone with him, his night-black eyes stirring her insides so pleasurably, Hannah went to him, framing his face between her trembling hands, hardly able to believe that she could be so bold, so reckless. She brought his lips to hers.*

*When his arms pulled her against his iron-hard body, his head swam with the ecstasy of the moment. Strong Wolf whispered against her lips "You want to see the horses now?" His fingers stroked her back. The heat of his touch reached through the thin fabric of her cotton blouse.*

*"Later" Hannah whispered back, her voice unfamiliar to her in its huskiness. Strong Wolf whisked her up into his arms and*

*held her close as their eyes met in unspoken passion. He kicked the door shut, then kissed her feverishly as he carried her towards his bed.*

An awful lot of whispering going on. I must learn to whisper more. And why do they always have names like Strong Wolf, never anything like John or Ted or Herbie or... Drew.

*Comanche by Fabio*

*She was tired of fighting him. She curled her arms around his neck and let herself succumb, only a little, to the potent feeling White Wolf's nearness aroused. He trailed warm kisses down her jaw, the curve of her neck. Then she felt his hot breath and wet lips tickling her. Maggie moaned softly. She had never known such rapture could exist. The intensity of the pleasure racked her with chills. With a devastating urgency, her resistance faded.*

*Maggie felt free of her shadow of control. Her heart hammering, her flesh crying out for her husbands heed, she mused that she might be out of her mind, and she was in the arms of a wild, totally aroused savage, determined to have her.*

Strong Wolf, White Wolf. They must be brothers. The Wolf brothers. They live just down the block. Sounds like Hannah and Maggie could be related too. It seems they both have a fondness for "totally aroused savages," but then, who doesn't?

*Song of a Warrior by Georgina Gentry*

*Passions flamed! "Green eyes, you are too innocent to know what might happen if I stay." Her heart skipped a beat. She was playing with fire, like a small child, suspecting the danger but too fascinated by the flame to back away while there was still time. Her whole being seemed controlled by heat and she couldn't control her words. "Don't go," she said again.*

*With a muttered curse, Bear turned and swept her into his embrace, holding her close against his powerful body. Willow knew she couldn't stop him now even if she wanted to. She was horrified when she realized she didn't want him to.*

Just another typical day on the Reserve. Bear and Willow at it again, sweeping and embracing everywhere. I tried sweeping and embracing once. The woman thought I was going for her purse. I couldn't walk properly for a week.

*Shawney Moon by Judith E. French*

*When his Shawney mother died, handsome half-breed Sterling Gray left the noble tribe that raised him and crossed an ocean to become a British soldier and gentleman. Now he's returning to his homeland with a breathtaking new bride. A Scottish hellion, wearing an ancient Celtic necklace, whom he rescued from a hangman's noose. Though his very presence inflames Caitlin's heart with a vengeful fire, Sterling knows the dangerous beauty is his destiny. A love foretold in mystic visions, a love for which he must risk his passions, his pride, and his future to win.*

I'm a half-breed. I've been to England—well actually, it was three hours in the Heathrow airport, but it was still England. Yet, for the life of me, I don't remember running across any Scottish hellions during my breakfast. Must have been an off day for them.

All things said and done, someday Lee and I will get this book off the ground. Is the world ready for it? Who knows? The world's just getting used to us not being stoical and silent, I don't know if it's ready for a little First Nations' slap and tickle.

And what should we call the book of Aboriginal ardour? Again Lee and I argued. My suggestion? I want to call it *The Night was Dark and so was He/She.*

# It's Alive

It's generally believed that contemporary Native theatre, as we know it today, began on November 26, 1986. On that auspicious day, a little play by an unknown playwright opened at the Native Canadian Centre, otherwise known as the Friendship Centre, in Toronto, Ontario. It was a harbinger of things to come.

That play was *The Rez Sisters*, and that playwright was Tomson Highway. At that time he was perhaps one of only two or three working Native playwrights in Canada, and the first whose work would reach outside of the Native universe to have larger repercussions in the Canadian theatrical community. Today I could easily name two to three dozen Native playwrights of produced and published work in Canada. If this rate of increase is maintained, I estimate that everybody in Canada will be a Native playwright by the year 2050.

With that in mind, I am delighted to report that in recent months there have been two milestones in the ongoing growth of Canadian Aboriginal theatre. Ironically, the first has to do with the final product of the playwright's process—the produced and staged play. The second has to do with the preparation for that particular journey—the playwright's education. And it's difficult to have one without the other.

Winnipeg native (no pun intended) Ian Ross won the 1997 Governor General's Award for Drama, one of the highest, if not the highest, honour for Canadian playwrights. The award was for his play *fareWel*, making him the first Native person to win a Governor General's Award, though Native writers like Tom King, Tomson Highway, and Daniel David Moses have all been nominated.

*fareWel* is an intense yet humourous slice of Reserve life as seen through the eyes of some wonderfully original characters. More importantly, it's an example of how far contemporary Native theatre has come since its inception all those years ago. The concept of a play written by, about, and for Native people was once the exception, but is now accepted as part of the mainstream. More than accepted; rewarded, in fact.

Meanwhile, a little further east, again in the fair city of Toronto, the next step in the evolution of Native theatre is taking form. In its twenty-fifth year of operation, the Native Theatre School (NTS), run by the Centre for Indigenous Theatre (CIT), is expanding and forging new paths.

For the past quarter century, CIT has operated a summer theatre school (NTS) dedicated to the training and growth of Native actors. Students spend their summers learning theatrical techniques combined with traditional Aboriginal teachings; the result is a unique training environment. The school's esteemed alumni includes Tina Keeper, Graham Greene, and Gary Farmer, to name only a few.

This year, like every year, the NTS is bringing together Native students from all over the continent for a two-month, intensive instructional period, taking place on a farm located several hours north of Toronto. In this rural setting, the concept of the "Four Directions" is stretched to the limit, with Native participants arriving from every corner of the continent.

For example: An Alaskan Aleut will be joining the school, all the way from California. A Cree will be in attendance, arriving from Nova Scotia, as well as a Plains Cree from Scarborough, near Toronto. A Micmac from London, Ontario, is also joining the group. And then there's the Manitoba Métis from Vancouver. And my favorite is the Ojibway who grew up near Martha's Vineyard, on Long Island, New York.

But, for the first time, the Native Theatre School is taking the next step in its progression into the next century by offering students a more comprehensive program called the Indigenous Theatre School Full-time Program. The ITS is for those whose interests in Native theatre and acting run deeper and longer than two summer months. Its aim is to develop contemporary performance art from distinctively Native cultural foundations over a longer period of time. The training program acts as a springboard from Native culture to contemporary theatre techniques and media training in such a way that the students will receive a uniquely Native beginning to their

144

performance arts career.

The curriculum integrates training in the areas of acting, voice, and movement, with Native cultural classes in dance, song, and oral history. And to gain practical performance experience, students will perform at the end of each semester in shows yet to be devised. (ITS will run from September till the end of April, during the standard school year; applications are accepted until the end of May, before the next Fall start date.)

There's the Dreamspeakers Aboriginal Film Festival, the Aboriginal Achievement Awards, the Three Fires Music Festival, and now the Indigenous Theatre School. A good friend once told me that Louis Riel has been quoted as saying "My people will go to sleep for a hundred years, and when they awake it will be the artists that will give them their spirit." I think I just heard the alarm go off.

# Book Tour Survivor

Book tours and readings. They can be an author's best friend: you sell oodles and oodles of books, allowing you, as a Canadian writer, the option of ordering a better class of cable television. Or they can be your worst nightmare: you sell no books and lose your precious television.

Seven books and many tours later, by some bizarre miracle, I still have not lost the urge to write, though I suffer from a clinical term referred to as BTS—Book Tour Syndrome. Trust me, I know the pain; I'm a book tour survivor. I'm thinking about starting up a support group. The syndrome is characterized by these symptoms: a lack of sleep due to continuous one-night stands (but, unfortunately, not the fun kind), far too much travel in too short a time, and a really bad diet caused by the incessant travel. Is it any wonder writers have a reputation for heavy drinking?

As Murphy's Law dictates—and I must first add that Murphy wrote this law and therefore must be classified as a writer—that whatever can go wrong, will go wrong. This is especially true of a book tour. Again, I'm a survivor, so I can prove it. Case in point: on one tour I was travelling from a reading in Regina to Calgary via a small commuter plane. Once there, I was to catch a connecting flight to Edmonton to do a subsequent reading. Somewhere high above the Prairies, the pilot made an announcement on the intercom. He cleared his throat a few times, then told us that "Due to mechanical difficulties, the plane was opting to land for an unscheduled stop in Medicine Hat."

The sudden and nervous looks from the other passengers mirrored my own. Mechanical difficulties. Two truly ominous words, especially at 20,000 feet. I had sudden images of Buddy Holly, Patsy Cline, Lynard Skynard, Rick Nelson, and a host of other singers whose planes had suffered "mechanical difficulties." Luckily, I could not come up with one single Native playwright/writer that had perished in such a circumstance—yet. For the first time in my life, I was grateful I wasn't a rock star.

We landed safely at the Medicine Hat airport, which, by the way, was closed on this wintry Sunday—meaning no food and no personnel until a new plane was flown in a few hours later. As it turned out, something was wrong with the previous plane's air conditioning. It was November. You wouldn't think this would be an issue.

As a result of this excitement, I ended up missing my flight to Edmonton, and had to wait a further two hours for the next one. Once in the air again, finally en route to the fair city of Edmonton, I was told we would be landing in the first big blizzard of the year. Huge snowdrifts and blowing snow made the landing and the trip into town a little difficult. Visions of the cab being blown into a snowdrift and me eating the cabdriver to survive until the spring thaw came, dogged my imagination. But being a trooper, I rushed from the cab, crawled over a growing snowdrift, and made my way into the bookstore, only ten minutes late, ready for my reading. There were three people there. One was a friend who was obligated. One was a photographer. He too was obligated.

Later that night, I was scheduled to read at a Métis Jamboree somewhere on the outskirts of Edmonton. I showed up, ready and willing to dazzle them with my literary repartee. First notice of a potential problem: it was a bar. A busy, crowded bar. A country band was wailing away in full country mode. People were dancing and drinking. Big cowboy hats and even bigger belt buckles were everywhere. It was basically a honky-tonk party. Something deep-down inside me said that these people probably, more than probably—I'd say almost positively—weren't exactly in the mood for a play reading. Images of the country bar scene from *The Blues Brothers* movie burst into my consciousness. Only I didn't see any chicken wire.

More recently, I was requested to do a reading at the Chapters store in downtown Toronto. I showed up, all eager and excited, prepared to burn the place down with my hot verbal wit. One problem: someone evidently forgot to advertise the presence of my hot verbal wit. Or more horrifying, maybe someone did and nobody cared because… nobody was there for the reading. Empty. Desolate.

Further Adventures of a Blue-Eyed Ojibway

Silent. Off in the distance, I thought I could hear a coyote howling. It was quite humbling.

But there is only one thing worse than nobody showing up for your reading. That's when just one or two, even three, people show up, and expect you to still do the reading. That's when you feel really uncomfortable. You're giving your all in a reading, knowing that one person out there is listening. You don't want to cheat them but you can't help thinking, "One person! Only one person. That's all?! I'm reading up here for thirty or forty minutes. And if I'm lucky, one person may, may, buy one whole book!" I think the down payment on that Lamborghini is still a little way down the road.

In all fairness, these make up the negative side of life in the touring trenches. I have also had many wonderful and fun things happen at readings. Luckily the good experiences outweigh the bad. That's why I still love doing them. They can be a great opportunity to introduce the public to some new work you are doing, and a chance to meet new friends, hopefully sell some books, and do some free travelling. Who can argue with that?

Still, the spectre of the Book Tour Syndrome continues to haunt me. I still have the nightmares. Occasionally I hear voices. Voices that have actually said stuff like "I'm a really big fan of yours. I just love your stuff. Really I do. My favourite is that short story you wrote about you and your brother taking your dead father home in a coffin through a snowstorm. That really touched me."

"That's wonderful," I remember saying to this sincere woman, "I'm really delighted. But I didn't write that. That's *Brothers in Arm*s by Jordan Wheeler."

But then again, I've done enough of these things that I don't remember my stuff anymore. I've lost track of everything I've written. Maybe I did write that one. Could Jordan Wheeler please let me know?

Printed and bound
in Boucherville, Quebec, Canada by
MARC VEILLEUX IMPRIMEUR INC.
in October, 1999